The Oratorio in Venice

ROYAL MUSICAL ASSOCIATION MONOGRAPHS

General editor: David Fallows

This series is supported by funds made available to the Royal Musical Association from the estate of Thurston Dart, former King Edward Professor of Music in the University of London. The editorial board is the Proceedings Committee of the Association.

ROYAL MUSICAL ASSOCIATION
MONOGRAPHS
2

The Oratorio in Venice

DENIS and ELSIE ARNOLD

Royal Musical Association
London
1986

Published by the Royal Musical Association,
Registered office c/o Waterhouse & Co., 4 St Paul's
Churchyard, London EC4M 8BA

© The Royal Musical Association 1986

British Library Cataloguing in Publication Data

Arnold, Denis
   The oratorio in Venice.—(Royal Musical
   Association monographs; 2)
   1. Oratorio—Italy
   I. Title   II. Arnold, Elsie   III. Series
   783.3'09   ML3233
   ISBN 0 947854 01 0

Typeset by Alan Sutton Publishing Limited, Gloucester
Music examples by Lincoln Castle Music Publications

Printed in Great Britain
Design and production in association with
Alan Sutton Publishing Limited, Gloucester

Copies may be obtained from:

RMA Secretary (members)   Brian Jordan (agent)
5 Church Street   or   12 Green Street
Harston   Cambridge
Cambridge   CB2 3JU
CB2 5NP

Contents

Preface

The history of the Italian oratorio is still known only rather sketchily in spite of the general studies of the genre by Arnold Schering and Howard Smither. In particular its popularity in Venice has been underestimated, probably because the composers who worked there often came from elsewhere and there is thus no school which can properly be called 'Venetian'. Nevertheless the sheer number of oratorio performances there was so large that the Serenissima was clearly a major centre; and the collection of scores preserved at the Fava church is so extensive that a considerable contribution to the history of the oratorio is possible. The gaps in this history can be filled to a certain extent by the examination of contemporaneous works given particularly in Vienna and Modena; and it seemed worth while to discuss these since they too are overlooked in the general histories. It also seemed worth while to compile a list of oratorios given in the Republic of Venice since Zorzi's original study is now out of date and in any case difficult to get hold of; and the long-awaited catalogue by Sven Hansell will be of a larger scope than is necessary here.

A list of singers, derived mainly from librettos, is included because it may help to date a great deal of Venetian church music, the manuscript scores of many items giving the names of the performers.

We should like to thank the librarians and staff of the Bayerische Staatsbibliothek in Munich, the Österreichische Nationalbibliothek in Vienna, and the Biblioteca Nazionale Marciana in Venice; Dr Alessandra Chiarelli of the Biblioteca Estense at Modena; but most of all Padre Mario Catapan of the Fava church who was extraordinarily kind; and Dr Margherita Obici Meneglietti of the Biblioteca Casa di Goldoni in Venice for her invaluable assistance.

Note

Oratorio titles mentioned in the text are normally followed by the serial number given to them in the Appendix, thus: *Sedecia* [1]. Currency is always a difficult subject, but in the documents cited here the lira = 20 piccoli (p); the ducat of account = 6 lire 4p; and the scudo = 9 lire 12p.

1
The Seventeenth Century

The oratorio arrived rather late in Venice. As usual. Venice, in music as in politics, was rarely in the forefront of development. It preferred to put a toe in the water and then, if the temperature seemed reasonable, to go (plunge would certainly be too strong a word) a little farther. But if convinced that it had found the way, its strength lay in its ability to build upon others' foundations and in its tenacity in holding to the genre or style – or committee structure – which it had so cautiously examined. Even its most famous musical device, the famed *cori spezzati* which was once believed to be the invention of Willaert, the *maestro di cappella* of St Mark's, now seems a development of a technique developed generally in Northern Italy; its individual Venetian usage came into being only after Andrea Gabrieli had spent some significant years in Munich.

So it was with the oratorio. It was not just a musical matter. The oratorio was the invention of the Oratorians, the order of St Philip Neri. This was essentially a Counter-Reformation movement, designed to bring the Church more immediately into the life of the common man. The order's Roman beginnings date back to the 1550s. It arrived in Venice only around 1660. Venice was never the spearhead against the Protestants. Indeed, after the Papal interdict of 1606, it had little love for Rome; at one time it even flirted with Protestantism itself. It actively disliked that other Counter-Reformation order, the Jesuits. Small wonder that the gentler Filippini were not tempted earlier, even though their movement was quite strong elsewhere in Italy.

Still, about 1660 they came. The details of their coming are unknown. The removal of an organ in August 1660 from S. Gregorio seems to indicate that they had settled temporarily there;[1] but they clearly wanted a home of their own, preferably near the centre of the city. In 1662 the Venetian Senate granted them the use and ownership of the oratory church of S. Maria della Consolazione (the Fava), very near the Rialto.[2] Today, its size can be seen only from the white tiles circumscribing the *terra sacra* in the campo at the front of the

---

[1] Venice, Archivio di Stato [ASV], Filippini, Busta 68, entry for 24 August 1660.
[2] Andrea da Mosto, *L'Archivio di Stato di Venezia: indice generale, storico, descrittivo ed analitico* (Rome, 1932).

present church. It was not very large; but it was by no means insignificant. Sansovino's guide book tells us:[3]

The oratory of S. Maria della Fava, which has more correctly the title of S. Maria di Consolatione, was first a little chapel, in which was painted the image of Our Lady, working miracles by revelation to the wife of one Francesco Amadi; in the year 1480, it was expanded [edificiò il luogo]. At first were created six procurators – three noblemen and three citizens – including among this number members of the Amadi family who, entrusted with the care of the church of S. Lio, put a chaplain in charge. Today [1581] it is made noble by beautiful and rich gold ornaments painted by Paolo Veronese, and by Benedetto his brother, both the altarpiece and the ceiling.

For the next year or so the Oratorians were clearly putting their new house in order, and we hear little of music, although the organ they had taken, being in bad condition, was put right at a cost of 68 lire. In 1661 they hired musicians for at least one 'solennità di Chiesa'.[4] But then, in 1663, their ceremonial suddenly flourishes.[5]

9 March for the solemnity in church 234 lire 9p, as follows. To Maestro Martin for the decorations [il Concier] 30 lire including 6 lire for the boat. To Signor Padre Nadal for the music 202 lire 12p; for a bunch of flowers [mazetto] for the Patriarch 37p. All this for the solemnity of St Philip Neri; and this was the first time that this solemnity was celebrated.

The fathers were pleased with themselves. In their minute book, they record: 'In conformity with already established custom was solemnised the first feast of our Holy Father with great devotion and a great throng of people, by the most exquisite music of Signor Maestro Don Natale Monferrato in all three of the functions of Vespers and sung Mass.'[6]

They had done well. Monferrato was *vicemaestro di cappella* at St Mark's and probably brought with him the choir and instruments (or some of them) of the basilica, as was the custom at other institutions throughout the city.[7] He was one of the most popular and fluent composers in Venice at the time. More important still for the present purpose was the fact that he was also the director of music at the Ospedale dei Mendicanti, and had been since 1642,[8] which surely explains how the fathers of the Oratory had found him. For the one certain set of friends they must have had on arriving in Venice was

---

[3] Francesco Sansovino, *Venetia città nobilissima*, ed. Giustiniano Martinioni (Venice, 1663), p.137 [reprint of early editions dating back to 1581, with additions for 1580-1663].

[4] ASV, Filippini, Busta 68, entry for 4 September 1661.

[5] Ibid., entry for 9 March 1663.

[6] Archive of the Fava, Libro de Decreti I, fol.1.

[7] Denis Arnold, 'Music at the Scuola di San Rocco', *Music and Letters*, xl (1959), pp.229-41.

[8] Giuseppe Ellero, *Arte e musica all'Ospedaletto* (Venice, 1978).

the membership of the Confraternity of St Philip Neri. This had been founded in 1621 and was still going strong forty years later. From the regulations[9] it is difficult to discover exactly what it was: it certainly included lay persons and, since some officials celebrated Mass, we must assume priests as well. In fact these rules, with their annual elections of officers, the duties to attend on a number of holy days, and the good works both of charity and of helping in the hospital, indicate that it was very like other Venetian confraternities, such as the *scuole grandi*. They had a room in the Mendicanti (now the Ospedale Civile) and there was some music at their meetings: Chapter 18 of the rules tells us that the 'coristi' must 'far intuonare li Salmi, Antifone, ed altro, secondo l'uso dell'Oratorio, due per parte, procurando d'intuonare alternativamente'; while Chapter 3, concerning the methods of conducting festivities, says that at the end of Mass, 'si canterà a due cori sempre, l'Inno *Te Deum laudamus*'. The extracts are best left in Italian, from which 'due cori' might imply something quite grand after the manner of the *cori spezzati* at St Mark's. 'Intuonare . . . due per parte' suggests plainsong – or at least quite simple music. In any case, it can hardly have been as sophisticated as the Oratorian fathers were used to in Rome and elsewhere. So no doubt meeting Monferrato was a convenient pleasure, and over the next few years they employed him to organise music on their saint's day and, from 1664, on the Feast of the Visitation of the Blessed Virgin, who was, as the paybook puts it, 'Titolo della Chiesa'.[10] They also began employing other musicians for other festivals, notably one Fra Paolo della Servi for the feast of the Madonna in July 1666.[11] Perhaps Monferrato, a very busy man, could not cope with the increase in festivals.

By this time, music was becoming considerably more important at the Fava. The fathers were much occupied in saying Masses for the dead, being left legacies for the purpose which they then invested for continued income. While it would take a prolonged investigation to follow their progress, there can be no doubt that they became rich quite quickly. There were perhaps a dozen fathers living together in a building attached to the church (monastery seems too grand a term). They gradually acquired property in and around the church, and by 1667 they had a new oratory. 'The new Oratory being near to completion . . . it is resolved to give oratorios [oratorj] in music, when the new Oratory is in order,' says a resolution of 6 October 1667.[12] On 5 December the minute book reports: 'In spite of the convenience of the new Oratory yesterday, which was the second Sunday in Advent, there was given the first oratorio in music,

[9] *Ordini che osservar si devono dalli divoti fratelli del pio oratorio di San Filippo Neri*, Venice, Biblioteca Nazionale Marciana, Misc. 132.11

[10] ASV, Filippini, Busta 68, entries for 2 July 1663; 26 May and 4 July 1664; 16 August 1665; 23 May 1666; 27 May and 2 July 1667.

[11] Ibid., entry for 3 July 1666.

[12] Fava Archive, Libro de Decreti I, fol.6.

certainly with a great crowd, but with diverse difficulties and a great deal of expense.'[13]

The first oratorio in music! Was it what we would mean by 'oratorio'? Or was it an elaborately sung Vespers? It might well be the former, which was, after all, a genre known to the fathers in Rome; and, as we shall see, the repertoire of such music was in circulation throughout Roman Catholic Europe. Anyway the paybook tells us of the 'great deal of expense': '4 December [1667]. For music in the Oratory 122 lire 14p, paid to the musicians for two oratorios in music, thus two Sundays, one being the second Sunday of Advent, which was the first day, and the other the third Sunday of Advent'.[14] Then a fortnight later '17 December. 62 lire 8p, given to the musicians for the oratorio given on the fourth Sunday of Advent'.

Christmas gone and oratorios became all the rage: New Year's Day, Epiphany, first and third Sundays after Epiphany, Septuagesima, 'giovedì grasso' (the Thursday before Lent), five during Lent, and two other occasions on which the music is specified as 'in the Oratory' rather than 'oratorio in music'. In charge of this music-making was a Signor Zuanne Pesarin, otherwise unknown to music history, who did very nicely out of this activity, getting an individual fee of 155 lire 'for the oratorios of the past winter' on 28 April, as well as, no doubt, his percentage as 'fixer' for each individual occasion. Nor was he engaged just in the Oratory. 26 May saw him paid for the Feast of St Philip Neri in the Oratorians' church, 2 July similarly for the Feast of the Visitation. On the Feast of the Assumption he provided a 'messa cantata' and 'the oratorio after 6 o'clock [dishor]'. The following year, the treasurer does not even bother to itemise the expenditure: '7 April [1669] for Music in the Oratory, 372 lire for the Oratorios in Music of this Lent, this month five Sundays at 12 ducats a time'.

Sixty ducats in all! Not perhaps a great amount for St Mark's, the state church; but probably a great deal more than any other church in Venice, whose habits were either to make do with their choir of resident monks or perhaps to hire some singers for the day of their patron saint. Noticeable also is the time: Lent, when the theatres were shut and church music elsewhere was on the whole less elaborate. Doubtless, there was always a 'great crowd'. Doubtless, also, there was more grumbling about the expense among the fathers. But their discontents were halted by a new arrival. The minute book records: '25 May 1669. At the meeting of the fathers in the usual place, it was proposed to be accepted among them Signor Don Giuseppe Uliasse, priest, Doctor of Laws and professor of music, a native of Ripa Transone in Romagna; and, after a debate, this was agreed.'[15] Sensibly they soon made him *prefetto della musica*, and music

---

[13] Ibid.

[14] This entry and subsequent ones are from ASV, Filippini, Busta 68, under dates.

[15] Fava Archive, Libro de Decreti I, fol.9.

flourished. In 1670 they had five oratorios during Lent at about the same cost: Pesarin looked after the celebrations of St Philip Neri and the Madonna.

The following year, a new name appears.[16]

15 March [1671] for music in the oratory 355 lire 12p for five oratorios on the first five Sundays of Lent. This not including payments to Maestro Signor Legrenzi nor the soprano from the household of the Most Illustrious Signor Baron Tasso who came continually several times at the instance of the maestro: this cost being 44 lire 12p for the first [oratorio], 66 lire 6p the second, 53 lire 18p the third, 115 lire 19p the fourth, and 75 lire 6p for the fifth, that are in all   355 lire 12p

At the end of the month there is a payment to Signor Maestro Legrenzi of 12 lire 8p 'as another present for the feast days, being household goods'. The domestic bursar's accounts carry on the tale:[17]

1 February [1672]
For Signor Maestro Legrenzi local red wine in 11 demijohns [mastelli] to the value of   104 lire

13 July
2 barrels [bijonzi] of wine to the Reverend Legrenzi   60 lire

Nor was it only wine. The previous year's bills with the confectioners include

22 February [1671]
For a basket of cakes [confecion] sent from the Arze and then sent to Maestro Legrenzi for Carnival   12 lire 8p

and 31 March

To Signor Maestro Legrenzi veal [vedello] weighing a quarter and 50 eggs in payment for a portrait of St Philip not in the current account   16 lire

They also bought his printed works:

21 January [1671]
A cecchino for a printed collection of Masses and Psalms by Father Don Gio Legrenzi   17 lire 5p

which must surely have been the *Sacri e festivi concenti, Messa e salmi a 2 cori con stromenti a beneplacito* published by Magni in 1667. Finally, the copyist's bills reveal Legrenzi's services to the fathers:

[16] ASV, Filippini, Buste 68 I and 68 II, entry under date.
[17] ASV, Filippini, Busta 63, entries under dates.

[1671]

5 March for copies of an oratorio *Sedecia* [1]	9 lire 10p
18 March for the copies of the *Oratorio della passione* [2]	7 lire 12p

and there are more payments for music unspecified.[18] In 1672 he was given four 'soppressa' (a type of salami), a kid and fifty eggs on 30 April to the value of 17 lire;[19] while a copyist in the same month was given 6 lire 5p for copies of *Moisè* [6] and 5 lire more for the oratorio *Creation del mondo* [4].[20] 1673 saw more wine sent to Legrenzi with, on 28 December, 'confectionery, a basket with two jars of mustard'; and so on until 1676.[21]

The general accounts fill in the details of repertoire and musicians employed. The accounts for 1672 are especially revealing. They begin to mention music in February when 'the new organ' arrived (payments to boatmen and porters on the 22nd and 23rd) and had to be paid for (396 lire 16p to the organ builder Father Anastasio from Vicenza on the 27th). Just in time for the oratorios of Lent.

13 March...for the oratorio *Moisè* [6]: 5 singers, 5 scudi; spinet, 9 lire 6p; bass lirone, 6 lire 4p; in all, 63 lire 10p

20 March...for 5 singers, 48 lire; theorbo and violone, 2 ducatoni [= 17 lire]; spinet, 1½d [=9 lire 6p]. Oratorio *Sedecia* [7]: 74 lire 6p

25 March...for 6 singers, 57 lire 12p; theorbo, 8 lire 10p; violone, 6 lire 4p; and spinet, 9 lire 6p. For the oratorio *Sisara* [8] with one singer in addition: 81 lire 12p

27 March...for 5 singers, 48 lire; theorbo, 8 lire 10p; violone, 6 lire 4p; spinet, 9 lire 6p. For the oratorio *L'huomo moribondo* [3]: 72 lire

31 March...for 7 singers, 67 lire 4p; violone, 6 lire 4p; spinet, 9 lire 6p. For the first oratorio on the 6th, *Creation del mondo* [4]: 82 lire 14p

3 April...for the *Oratorio della passione* [2]: 5 singers, 48 lire, plus another singer, 6 lire 4p; spinet, 9 lire 6p; violone, 6 lire 4p; theorbo, 8 lire 10p; gondola for the rehearsal, 1 lira: 79 lire 4p

[same day]

to Pesarin for the oratorio *L'huomo moribondo*, 9 lire 12p

5 April: oratorio of the Judgement [*Giudizio*; 5]: 8 singers, thus for 6, 57 lire 12p; another at 6 lire 4p; and the other was not paid since he was from the Cà Marcello; 2 violins, 12 lire 8p; viola, 4 lire 16p; theorbo and basso, 17 lire; spinet, 9 lire 6p: 103 lire 6p

---

[18] Ibid., fol.23v.
[19] Ibid., entry under date.
[20] Ibid., fol.59v.
[21] ASV, Filippini, Buste 62, 63, 64, 68 I and 68 II.

And this was only in Lent. There was much music throughout the rest of the year, but it was given in church and presumably was liturgical or paraliturgical in form.

Father Uliasse must surely have been responsible for such riches. He had also found a winner in Legrenzi. We know little about the composer's arrival in Venice except that it happened about 1670; and he became Monferrato's successor at the Mendicanti in 1672. He was in his forties with a wealth of experience in Ferrara, where he had been in charge of the music at one of the religious confraternities, the Accademia dello Santo Spirito; conditions at the Fava can have come as no surprise to him. He had also had some experience of opera, but seemingly had not yet achieved the fame of others: this was to come. Perhaps, indeed, he had decided to try in Venice to become an opera composer.

It is generally thought that he had written his oratorios for Ferrara, but the account books of the Fava prove that it was in fact a new genre for him around 1670; it was the success of his Venetian oratorios that ensured their performance elsewhere. Some of the oratorios mentioned in the account books cannot be firmly identified as his. Indeed, a present of fifty eggs was sent to 'Signor Maestro Ziani in Crepello' on 31 March 1671, surely for some services rendered.[22] Pietro Andrea Ziani was, in fact, the only Venetian with any real experience of composing oratorios, having been in Vienna since the 1660s and having written at least three for the imperial court. That said, the energy and fluency of Legrenzi is remarkable. Even if we accept as Ziani's contribution *Il cuore humano all'incanto* [15] of 1673, Legrenzi still composed five oratorios in the seasons 1671-5; and maybe more. The works which must surely be ascribed to him are: 1671, *Sedecia* [1]; 1672, *Sisara* [8] and *Giudizio* [5]; 1673, *La morte del cor penitente* [11]; 1675, *Gli sponsali d'Ester* [20]. (To these must possibly be added *La vendita del cuor humano* [15], given in 1673 and repeated the following year, if it was not in fact the work of Ziani.) They can be identified from librettos for performances given in 1676 and 1677 in Ferrara.

There are several other candidates for Legrenzi's authorship: *S. Giovanni Battista* [13], *Adamo et Eva* [16], and a work with an illegible title, all given in 1673 and 1674 and not found elsewhere; the fact that no other composer appears in the fairly full records of the Fava at this time (Pesarin, who was eventually to become *maestro di cappella* to the fathers, has left no sign of composition) suggests that Legrenzi may have composed some if not all of them also. This is the more remarkable since he can have had few models on which to base his own work. The Emilian school to some degree perhaps; but its glorious days were those of Duke Francesco II of Modena in the 1680s, to which even Stradella's great oratorio *S. Giovanni Battista* belongs. The Oratorian fathers probably knew of Roman develop-

---

[22] Ibid., Busta 63, entry under date.

ments since members of the community were frequently going to Rome. There even appears a payment to one Signor Ieppo Carissimi Musico, for having sung 'many times at the usual functions';[23] while in 1675 the treasurer paid 'the remainder for the copies of the oratorio from Bologna, 13 lire 3p'. Such foreign connections were unusual in the musical life of Venice, which tended to be rather inward-looking, at times even parochial. Nonetheless, it was Legrenzi's gifts which established the genre in Venice.

Smither has pointed out that most of Legrenzi's extant oratorios deal with biblical stories, the others being on allegorical or 'mystery'-type themes.[24] The inference might be drawn that the trend was towards an operatic style; and indeed his analysis of *Sedecia* [1] tends to confirm this.[25] While it still has a *testo*, or narrator, the two protagonists, Zedekiah and Nebuchadnezzar, are differentiated in music; and there are choruses for Zedekiah's soldiers and the Chaldean army. Yet one must doubt whether Legrenzi saw the oratorio as a dramatic affair – or indeed whether drama was even his main interest in opera itself. It is worthy of notice that two manuscripts of arias from his operas, no doubt intended for use in noble houses,[26] show that he was a writer of tunes. He arrived at opera at a time when the aria had very nearly conquered. True, Alessandro Scarlatti had yet to come. And certainly, *Sedecia* is not just a succession of arias; it takes in some ensembles (including attractive duets for the soprano 'figlioli di Sedecia') and two of the grand madrigal-finales of the kind that Luigi Rossi had used in his Roman oratorios.

Still, from examination of the score of *La vendita del cuor humano* [15],[27] it is obvious that it was not the plot or the dramatic elements in the music that ensured its success. The conception is very suitable for the limited resources of the Fava. There are two characters, the 'Cuor humano' (S) and the Angel (A), who sing throughout; Piacer (T) and Mondo (B) turn into the Demon (B) and Jesus (T) in the second part. There are no instruments apart from the continuo, hence no overture or ritornellos. There are many pieces marked 'aria' for the complete cast (though when the tenor becomes Jesus he sings only in arioso). Both parts end with a quartet, each marked 'madrigale' in the Vatican score,[28] far more complex in musical texture and emotional variety than the 'coro' finales to become common in the eighteenth century, but with much the same purpose. These fixed 'numbers' are set within a continuous flow, moving smoothly into recitative or arioso.

---

[23] Ibid., Busta 64, entry for 10 June 1677.
[24] Howard E. Smither, *A History of the Oratorio*, i (Chapel Hill, 1977), p.310.
[25] Ibid., pp.310-14.
[26] In particular in Venice, Accademia Querini-Stampalia, ms 1430, arias from *Totila*; ms 1432, arias from *Antioco il grande* and *Il Creso*; and many items in lesser anthologies.
[27] Modena, Biblioteca Estense, F.1544.
[28] Vatican City, Biblioteca Apostolica Vaticana, ms Chigi Q.VI.89.

There is evidence of more extended structures with repeated sections used after the manner of a rondo. And there is also a certain amount of 'characterisation'. The reason that Jesus never has an aria is surely that such grave figures must not be seen to be melodious. The Demon is a 'great bass' – or rather baritone – in a tradition which goes back to Charon in Monteverdi's *Orfeo* and forward to bass villains of the eighteenth century. But tunes are the thing. Some are typical of the mid-baroque bel canto, being smooth arias in 3/2. More often they are in that chattering syllabic style with a rhythm such as ♪♪ | ♪♪ ♪♪ ♩ dominating the piece in regular phrases, the words repeated ad libitum. The prevailing impression is of charm rather than power (in which Legrenzi differs from Carissimi or Luigi Rossi). Yet at times he can move: at the beginning of the second part, the human heart sings what might fairly be called a lament, 'Help, O you heavens my friends, the tears of a heart that is dying' (example 1). The chromatic bass, the suspensions and the augmented-sixth harmonies make this more than just agreeable melody.

Ex. 1 Legrenzi: *La vendita del cuor humano*

As befits the subject, *La morte del cor penitente* [11] has more in similar manner than of cheerful tunes. It is on a large scale, at least as it appears in a score made for a performance at the Viennese court in the time of the Emperor Leopold.[29] There are just three singers: Peccatore (T), Penitenze (S) and Speranza (S), with a 'coro di pene'. But there is also a four-part string ensemble which not only plays *sinfonie* and ritornellos but also accompanies the voice extensively. This automatically tends to make the set pieces clearer in structure, for a ritornello suggests da capo or rondo forms. But in general there is still a fluent texture. Recitative is rarely just narrative but rather an expressive arioso. Words tend to be repeated to round off phrases. Expressive phrases suggest unusual harmonies or melodic snatches, as is evident from the opening arioso of the sinner, immediately after

---

[29] Vienna, Österreichische Nationalbibliothek, Musiksammlung, ms Leopoldina 18890.

Ex. 2 Legrenzi: *La morte del cor penitente*

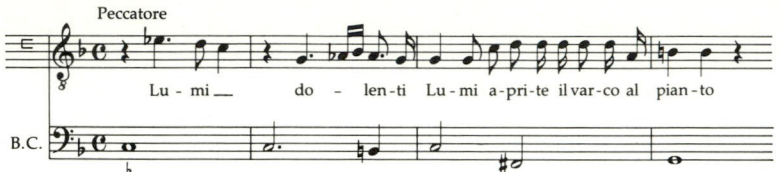

the overture (example 2). There are a number of 'bel canto' arias, usually long and with a touch of the operatic lament, sung generally by the Sinner (Peccatore). There are others in the syllabic, chattering style, while one in 6/8 is positively jolly; these are usually allocated to Hope (Speranza). The 'coro di pene', written for five voices (SSATB), takes part in a scene which is organised on an ample scale, the tutti used as a ritornello interspersed with solos and duets. The madrigal at the end of the first part is again a concertante piece after the Roman style; that at the end of the oratorio is even more elaborate and involves the strings.

We cannot be sure that the Vienna score represents the music heard in the Fava on the sixth Sunday of Lent 1673. String players are rarely mentioned in the accounts, though it must be said that the instrumental parts in the Vienna score seem totally idiomatic, and if they were not written by Legrenzi (dead nearly fifteen years before the Vienna performance) they were composed by somebody with a very good appreciation of his style. The account book merely says '25 March [1673]. 6° oratorio, *Peccator pentito* [12], Voci 6, 100 lire 12p'.[30] If this does not match the surviving score, it is surely too much of a coincidence that there should be two oratorios on such closely related themes.

In any case, the manner is clear. These oratorios of the 1670s are modest affairs, involving a small group of singers, a continuo group which includes a theorbo and a violone, perhaps an organ (there was a small one in the Oratory) and a spinet, and at times a quartet of strings. The cost was small, a matter of only 20 ducats at most – not the stuff which permitted the hiring of opera singers. And although we shall find that musicians were sometimes content to perform at the Fava for little or nothing (except, perhaps, the future comfort of their immortal souls) it is evident that the performers were more likely to be from St Mark's than from the Teatro S. Cassiano. These oratorios are in no sense showpieces for the performers. The soprano parts occasionally go up to a top G, and the bass parts sometimes involve some fioritura; that is about as far as virtuosity is taken.

We have seen that one singer was not paid for the performance of *Giudizio* [5] in 1672 because 'he came from the Cà Marcello', which implies that he was in the service of the Marcello family. On another occasion, the cost of putting on an oratorio was refunded by the

---

[30] ASV, Filippini, Busta 68, entry under date.

'noblewoman Contarini' to the tune of 124 lire.[31] The costs to the fathers were therefore light enough not to deter them: the growing number of legacies, to judge from the miscellaneous documents preserved today, were to make the community distinctly wealthy. But musical activities (like so many others) are dependent on the enthusiasms of particular men; and, from this point of view, disaster struck in 1676 when the Doge and Senate passed legislation against foreigners in religious orders. The fathers could no longer have Uliasse as their *prefetto della musica*, although 'if he should wish to serve in the house as organist, he shall be granted rights to the common table and his salary'.[32] If the analogy of an Oxford or Cambridge college might be used, he was thus deprived of his place on the governing body, even if he continued to live with the fathers and to say Masses for them. He seems not to have wanted to become their organist, for by January 1677 they decided formally to appoint one, a professional. The immediate favourite was Pesarin, but they obviously felt some embarrassment at the position of Legrenzi who might have expected to be considered; and they eventually decided to write to him expressing the hope that he would continue to provide oratorios as in the past even though Pesarin would be in charge of the music in general.[33] He seems to have accepted this. There were five oratorios in Lent 1677 and, on 31 December, wine to the value of 106 lire 2p was sent to 'Signor Maestro Legrenzi for the oratorios in music'.[34]

There was worse to come. On 18 August, the fathers were in an economical mood. They decreed that the expenditure on their principal festivals – St Philip Neri, the Visitation and the Assumption – should not exceed 60 ducats and that they 'must suspend for the present the oratorios given during Lent until further notice'.[35] Of the seven members of the governing body present, five agreed, two dissented. The oratorio clearly needed Uliasse's missing advocacy. Then on 9 December they dismissed all their musicians except for the organist, who was given 24 ducats a year (about the norm for organists at confraternities and lesser churches). There was some opposition yet to come. On 15 February 1679 'In view of the many requests, and also offers to provide the money for the Lenten oratorios, it was proposed to restart them…and the motion was lost, 3 white balls to 4 black'.[36] Grumpy were the fathers; and their resolution ended the first phase of the oratorio in Venice.

[31] Ibid., fol.56.
[32] Fava Archive, Libro de Decreti I, fol.34, 18 December 1676.
[33] Ibid., fol.41: 'Dovendosi far elezione di un Organista, ed assistente alla Musica fu ricordati, che v'erano in ciò alcune difficolta: penä di parola già data del Pre A. Ermanno allora Preposito al Signor Giovanni da Pesaro: secondo essere di presente impegnatadi col Signor Maestro Legrenzi per gli Oratorij [they decide to write to him saying that they want Pesarin as organist but] offerendogli gli Oratorij, e pregandola a favorire in quelli cose per il passato.'
[34] ASV, Filippini, Busta 64, fol.165.
[35] Fava Archive, Libro de Decreti I, fol.47.
[36] Ibid., fol.55.

No doubt the unwillingness of the fathers to continue with the oratorios was due to there being nobody capable – or with the will – to organise them. Without Uliasse, they had no enthusiast; and it was exactly at this time that Legrenzi began to become a success elsewhere. In 1676, *Sedecia* [1] and *La vendita del cuor humano* [15] were given at Ferrara, and *Gli sponsali d'Ester* [20] at Modena; the following year, *Ester* was performed at Ferrara. 1676 sees the start of his series of operas for the various Venetian theatres, at S. Giovanni Grisostomo in particular, one of the most important opera houses in the city. His income from the Mendicanti secure, his expectations and receipts from the opera houses increasing, there must have been little incentive for him to continue to work for the Fava, even though it provided him with enough wine for the year, and eggs and cakes at Christmas. In the event, he preserved his affections for the Oratorian fathers; he was buried in their ground (the exact place is now unknown) and left them a legacy from his quite opulent estate.

But if there was no one at the Fava to continue the tradition, the oratorio had clearly been a source of enjoyment and edification for many; and, as said, traditions survived tenaciously in Venice. There was no reason for other churches to take on the work. St Mark's plodded on its way, conforming to its grand ceremonial books, scarcely altered over the centuries.[37] The other churches celebrated their patron saints with music and perhaps provided music for Holy Week.[38] There was, nevertheless, a group of organisations which were not unlike the Fava, at least in possessing an outward attitude to the laity. These were the *ospedali*.

The famous period of the *ospedali*, at least as music schools, was to be the eighteenth century;[39] but recent researches suggest that they had taken music seriously long before.[40] In the earlier part of the seventeenth century, they generally found their music masters in the *cappella* of St Mark's. By 1680 they were branching out. Legrenzi himself had benefited by being appointed *maestro di musica* at the Ospedaletto in 1670, on his arrival in Venice and before he received either a post at St Mark's or profitable commissions from the theatres. But it is significant that in 1676, when activities at the Fava were diminishing (operas, however, being produced), he transferred to the Mendicanti where he remained until 1682; presumably his activities as *vicemaestro* at St Mark's were taking up his time.

Although apparently the Pietà was content with the old ways, the Incurabili found Carlo Pallavicino to direct their music. Pallavicino was a local boy to the extent that he had been born in Salò, on Lake Garda and hence Venetian *terra ferma*. He had Venetian connections,

---

[37] See James H. Moore, *Vespers at St. Mark's* (Ann Arbor, 1981).

[38] For example, the Salute; see ASV, S. Maria della Salute, Busta 86.

[39] See Denis Arnold, 'Orphans and Ladies: the Venetian Conservatoires (1680-1790)', *Proceedings of the Royal Musical Association*, lxxxix (1962-3), pp.31-47.

[40] Ellero, op. cit. (n. 8), pp.43 and 157.

no doubt, yet was no stay-at-home, for he had been at the Saxon court at Dresden, that most italianised of courts (Vienna not excluded) north of the Alps. He was an international figure, and was to return to Dresden after he had given the Incurabili eleven years between 1674 and 1685. An opera composer rather than a church musician, he was more advanced in style even than Legrenzi.

So it comes as no surprise to find oratorios being performed at the Incurabili in the 1680s. If they had brought a great throng of people to the Fava, they might well do the same for the *ospedale*, where the need for funds to support the poor, sick and old never diminished. In 1687 Pallavicino produced *Il trionfo dell'innocenza* [117], and two other oratorios were given in the following year, *Iberia convertita* [121] and *Maria Maddalena* [122]. These were days when few librettos were printed, and our information about performances is sketchy.[41] No scores survive; but at Modena, Pallavicino's *Il trionfo della castità* is to be found in the form of both libretto and score. The libretto was printed at Modena in 1688, though the title page does not divulge further information about a performance there: *Il Trionfo Della Castità, Oratorio del Dottore Giovanni Matteo Giannini Posto in Musica Dal Signor Carlo Pallavicini, Mastro di Capella de gl'Incurabili di Venezia*. The cast list is more revealing and surely indicates a Venetian origin, if not performance:

Testo	Soprano
Santa Genefa, moglie di	Soprano
Sifrido, palatino del Reno	Soprano
Alimondo, suo fratello	Soprano
Gloraspe, maggiordomo di Sifrido	Alto
Calunnia, che comparisce in sembianza	
di Eliza nutrice di Gloraspe	Alto
Innocenza	Soprano

with other parts which can be doubled by those above:

Maria Vergine	Soprano
Elvio camariere di Gloraspe	?
Castità	Soprano
Tentatione	Alto

What is this farrago of allegorical figures, Rhenish princes (Siegfried?) and household, disguised personages and female saints that still needs a *testo* or narrator? It is, of course, the confused Venetian opera of the 1680s, a fact confirmed by the note that 'The oratorio takes place near Trier' (not far from the Rhine). Do we already see the perspective scenes, and surely the Virgin Mary must

---

[41] *Pallade veneta*, a Venetian chronicle of events. The musical references will be published shortly in *Pallade veneta: Writings on Music in Venetian Society*, ed. Eleanor Selfridge-Field (Venice, 1985).

arrive on a cloud machine? Not quite. For if the disposition of parts reveals that all (except Elvio, perhaps) can be taken by girls and women, and if, as seems eminently possible, it was given at the Incurabili, there was neither room nor money for the extravagances of the opera house. It may, of course, have been different at Modena.

There can be no doubt of the nature of the music, as preserved in a score surely meant for the same performance as the libretto.[42] It is operatic in a way that Legrenzi's works are not. To the singers is added a four-part string ensemble; and one aria needs an obbligato trumpet. There are many arias, some marked 'da capo' and at least one with the da capo written out; there is one over a descending ostinato bass; others are in the 'arietta' chattering style – all of which sounds as though it is near to Legrenzi. But the older 3/2 bel canto has gone and a more emotionally relevant style has come in. There seems more dramatic purpose in the arias, as in the 'revenge' aria of Alimondo, the opening of which is shown in example 3. The

Ex. 3 C. Pallavicino: *Il trionfo della castità*

'trumpet' aria is the forerunner of the military manner of many an eighteenth-century piece, although it may owe something to Antonio Sartorio who uses it in both opera and motets, and even more to the trumpet school of composers in Modena and Bologna. Indeed, the clear tonality of almost all the music reminds us that the 1680s are the era, par excellence, of Corelli, whose method of instant modulation was to infect the whole of Europe. Pallavicino's music is very up to date. The only piece which seems backward-looking in any way is the final love duet (example 4), with its reminiscences of Monteverdi's *L'incoronazione di Poppea*, though one notices that Monteverdi's sweetly paining dissonances have been replaced by mellifluous thirds and gentle hemiola.

With this quality of music, it was no surprise that Pallavicino returned to the lush pastures north of the Alps; and it is the more remarkable that *Il trionfo della castità* does not make extraordinary demands on the singers, with the exception of the 'trumpet' aria

[42] Modena, Biblioteca Estense, F.895.

Ex. 4 Ibid.

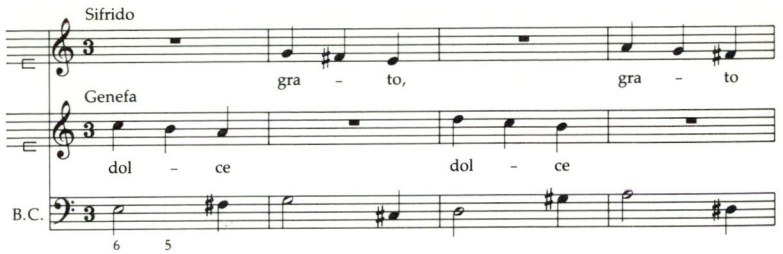

which, being marked 'musico' (often to be interpreted as castrato), might have been a concession to the taste of the Estensi. The time of virtuoso display had yet to come at the *ospedali*.

Were these works of Pallavicino, Spada's *Santa Maria egittiaca penitente* [423] given in 1687 at the Pietà, and one or two others, merely 'strays', or have our sources of information failed us? The temptation must be to think that there may have been other oratorios given around 1690, even though Venetian gossip and antiquarianism, in the form of Allacci's catalogue and the various manuscripts in the Marciana, reveal nothing. In any case, there was nothing at the Fava during these years: that is revealed by the order's minute book. Pesarin contented them with music for their holy days, and they kept the organ in the church in good order. Then, in 1693, there are signs of new life. On 23 December one Girolamo Finazzi 'sacerdote veneto' asked to be allowed to live in the house, offering to take charge of the music and pay the goodly sum of 100 ducats for his meals. The fathers knew and liked the said Don Girolamo, and agreed to 'a room and common table with the title of Director of Music'.[43] It can surely be no coincidence that on 25 April 1694 the fathers were reporting annoyance at the 'concorso del Popolo' which caused disturbance on the day of their patron saint; but the resolution to cut down on the music was lost.[44] Don Girolamo, however, could not persuade them the following January to 'riassumere gli Oratorij in Musica la sera' even though only one performance per year was proposed.[45]

He had not yet lost. On 3 February 1696 the matter was reconsidered:[46]

Having the universal desire that an oratorio in music should be given for a single evening at Lent at the end of Carnival, to give also to the brothers of the Oratory some devotional recreation: it is decided to do this, on the condition that several musicians are prepared to sing gratis. This was a unanimous decision.

A little later in the month, the fathers heard an application from one Signor Don Ascanio Belli to live with them. Belli had been a singer at St Mark's and, if the minute pitches it a bit high to say that he was a 'famoso musico e contralto', he had been in the service of the Duke of Parma; thus he was granted a room and common table 'in the same way as Signor Don Carlo [sic] Finazzi'.[47] The order was becoming musical again; and the oratorio was a success: '1 March. Having had the universal approbation of the oratorio in music given on the last Sunday of Carnival, the fathers decided that one should be repeated on the evening of Passion Sunday'.[48] The shortness of the time scale had not allowed for new works to be written. The accounts tell us that they had revived Legrenzi:[49]

1696
Function of the Oratory, paid on 17 April 1696 to Padre Bartolomeo Grilli 19 lire 14p for copies and the viola da spalla 1 ducat for the oratorio given on the last day of Carnival, when they gave *Il cuore humano* [26] with new additions and the part of the Angel   19 lire 14p

and

30 April on account of the oratorio *L'huomo moribondo* [27] on Passion Sunday, copies and viola da spalla   28 lire 14p

'New additions' were, of course, no novelty in the seventeenth century. The vicissitudes of such a score as *L'incoronazione di Poppea* as

---

[43] Fava Archive, Libro de Decreti I, fol.111.
[44] Ibid., fol.114.
[45] Ibid., fol.117.
[46] Ibid., fol.121.
[47] Ibid., fol.121.
[48] Ibid., fol.121.
[49] ASV, Filippini, Busta 68, entries under date.

it did the rounds of the theatres are well known. Nevertheless, to add to a work composed over twenty years earlier surely seems unsatisfactory, and one is a little relieved to find that new compositions were also forthcoming. One source records a performance of Vinacesi's *Il cuor nello scrigno* [25] on 4 March.[50] Of this there is no trace in either minute book or accounts of the Fava, and since they are unusually full at that time, it must be a matter for doubt. More likely is that it was given later in the year, for oratorio fever again infected the fathers. On 21 May they passed a resolution 'that the prefect of music should prepare six or seven oratorios in music for the coming winter to be sung, spaced out one each month, beginning at the end of November, each one, however, being given as economically as possible'.[51] And again, these were an enormous success, for the fathers thought the matter was getting out of hand by 8 January 1697.[52]

Several [fathers] have been disturbed that there was a repetition, on another evening of a ferial day, of the oratorio given on New Year's Day to universal applause, this being against the customs of the order, which decree similar oratorios on the evenings of festivals. It was resolved that, it not being possible to have oratorios on [all] festivals, it is not desired to have them on ferial days.

The following winter there was another season. On 5 December, the fathers agreed 'that there can be four or five oratorios in music, on condition that there should be no financial burden on the House, as in the previous year'.[53] The fathers do not seem to have had a composer-in-residence, so to speak, but a payment of 6 January 1699 'given to Ziani to give to Maggini for the cembalo and expenses 10 lire 10p'[54] suggests that Ziani may have been important to them; and some mysterious payments to him some years later,[55] apparently for standing in briefly for their permanent organist, offer further hints of his connection with the Fava. There must perforce have been other such occasions, and a minute of the fathers for 9 September 1698 gives an indication that they may have been rather grander affairs than had been expected. In a decree putting the prefect of music and Don Ascanio Belli in charge of the general arrangements of the oratorio season from November to Easter the fathers added the proviso that[56]

it shall not be permitted on Lenten evenings to recite oratorios with *sinfonie*, ritornellos or concertos with violins and violettas, but only with the basso

---

[50] *The New Grove Dictionary*, article 'Vinaccesi', by Sven Hansell.
[51] Fava Archive, Libro de Decreti I, fol.122.
[52] Ibid., fol.123.
[53] Ibid., fol.125.
[54] ASV, Filippini, Busta 68, fol.361.
[55] Ibid., Busta 64, fol.321.
[56] Fava Archive, Libro de Decreti I, fol.126.

continuo, and this to the satisfaction of the composer: it is permitted, however, for the prefect of music to allow several virtuosos whom he would wish to hear with various instruments, but only at the time after the sermon of the priest, at the beginning of the second part, and at no other time.

Of these new composers, it is noticeable that only Caldara was an inexperienced Venetian. Vinacesi, who became *maestro di coro* at the Ospedaletto in 1698,[57] was from Brescia and had connections with the Modena school. Marc'Antonio Ziani had been *maestro di cappella* at S. Barbara in Mantua, the ducal chapel of the Gonzagas. He had already had a dozen operas performed at the principal Venetian theatres and was soon to depart for Vienna, where he became Hofkapellmeister. These were not likely to see an oratorio as a small-scale devotional piece for the Filippini.

Indeed, if we look at Vinacesi's *Susanna* of 1694, preserved at Modena[58] and presumably meant for the Este court, we see a totally different attitude from that of Legrenzi in the 1670s. There is a five-part string band and it plays full-blown ritornellos indeed. The parts for the first violins are often very elaborate and difficult. One aria has obbligato parts for two solo cellos. The overture is a four-movement orchestral concerto, with a *moto perpetuo*-type presto as the third movement. The cast of two sopranos, an alto (for Susanna), tenor and bass (the two elders) needs at least one very good singer (Giachino) and two others of skill (Daniel and Susanna). Daniel, indeed, has a splendid 'judgement' aria and there is a love duet at the end for Giachino and Susanna 'Pace, pace, amata moglie'. The final number is a madrigal, not in the complex manner of the mid-seventeenth century but rather a 'coro' foreshadowing the eighteenth-century tradition, a *lieto fine* with a homophonic texture for the cast, doubled by the strings. This really is an opera in all but name, and the example (if not the downright influence) of Stradella comes to mind. The arias are grander in scale than those in the earlier oratorios, often da capo in form and of a dramatic force.

Vinacesi was to become a fixture in the Venetian scene, at the *ospedali* and at St Mark's; but, alas, he produced no corpus of oratorios. Caldara, a singer at St Mark's in 1698, was soon on his travels, like Ziani to Vienna where the pair of them did indeed provide an oratorio repertoire. Caldara's first piece for the Fava has disappeared, but his later work, for Vienna, survives. As it has received an excellent critical examination[59] it need not be considered here. Suffice to say that although such titles as *Il trionfo della continenza* [32] and *Il ricco epulone* [35] seem rather backward-looking, the surviving music itself is by no means always so. True, a particularly

[57] Ellero, op. cit. (n.8), p.43.
[58] Modena, Biblioteca Estense, F.1230.
[59] Ursula Kirkendale, *Antonio Caldara: sein Leben und seine venezianisch-römischen Oratorien* (Graz and Cologne, 1966).

expressive piece of arioso-cum-recitative, full of chromatics and strangely moving harmonies,[60] in *Il trionfo della continenza* belongs to the seventeenth-century tradition. The arias, on the other hand, seem to belong to the post-Scarlatti era, with longish phrases and sections based on strong, clear rhythms, almost in the manner of a minuet or gavotte (such as can be found in Handel's operas of the 1720s). The orchestra has a substantial part to play, so substantial that one wonders if this were not the sort of piece responsible for the fathers' decree forbidding the use of an instrumental ensemble; though it must be said that the scores which survive may have been intended for later performances.

After this burst of energy, the feast of oratorios at the Fava died out. There was no final resolution that the performances should cease; they just did not continue. The fathers did not neglect music. They had an organist, and a group of singers was engaged for the major festivals; but there were no oratorios. Perhaps Belli's energy ran out. He died in 1709 leaving an ample legacy to the church. The organist, Di Corte, was certainly a nonentity. Coronelli's guide book continued to advise visits to the Fava for its music;[61] but the church disappears from our story for just forty years, before returning in even greater glory.

[60] Ibid., p.235.
[61] *Guida de' Forestieri* (Venice, edition of 1706), p.67.

2
The Conservatories: 1700-1740

The fathers were, in fact, about to embark on the great venture of building a new church, the one which stands near the Rialto today. The *ospedali*, or conservatories, were at this time not involved in such expensive projects (those were to come later in the 1740s). Music was more important than ever to them. In 1700 Vinacesi was *maestro* at the Ospedaletto; Biffi at the Mendicanti; Lotti almost certainly at the Incurabili; while Francesco Gasparini was soon to be the new arrival at the Pietà. The first three, who spent years in the service of St Mark's, can fairly be called church musicians. But all except Biffi were also opera composers. Vinacesi had set *L'innocenza giustificata* in 1698 and would produce *Gli amanti generosi* for the Teatro S. Angelo in 1703. Lotti began work for the Teatro S. Cassiano with *Sidonio* in 1706 and thereafter was much involved with opera. Gasparini was the star. He had scarcely arrived in Venice when his *Tiberio imperatore d'oriente* was produced at the Teatro S. Angelo in 1702; and thereafter a huge stream of operas flooded forth until 1716, when he had departed to Rome. Indeed, we may suspect that Gasparini accepted the relatively modest stipend of 200 ducats from the Pietà as a sinecure while he earned real money from the Venetian opera houses.

Be that as it may, he did not do badly for the Pietà's governors. In many years they gave him a present of 50 ducats because, as they said, 'he has done his ordinary duties [admirably], not only in teaching the girls with great benefit to its music, but also in other ways, especially on the occasions of the Solemn Feasts and the Novena of Christmas with compositions universally much applauded'.[1] Oratorios are never mentioned in the governors' minutes but Gasparini had already composed in the 1690s at least two oratorios for the Filippini in Florence,[2] and we know from librettos that in most years he wrote one for the Pietà:

---

[1] ASV, Ospedali e luoghi pii, Busta 688, notatorio H, fols.40v-41.
[2] See Renzo Lustig, 'Saggio bibliografico degli oratorii stampati a Firenze dal 1690 al 1725', *Note d'archivio*, xiv (1937), pp.57-64, 109-16 and 244-50.

1701	*Triumphus misericordiae* [426]
1702	*Prima culpa per redemptionem deleta* [427]
1703	*Jubilum prophetarum* [428]
1704	*Aeterna sapientia incarnata* [429]
1705	*Pudor virginis vindicatus* [430]
1706	*Genus humanum* [431]
1706?	*Sol in tenebris* [432]
1708	*Dominicae nativitatis praeludium* [433]
1711	*Maria Magdalene videns Christum* [435]
1712	*Moisè liberato dal Nilo* [436]
1714	another version of *Maria Magdalene* [437]

The gap in 1713 may be accounted for by his leave of absence granted by the governors in September 1712;[3] the others, perhaps, simply by our loss of their librettos. After Gasparini's departure, Vivaldi continued the tradition until 1716; then it disappeared.

The *maestri* at the other *ospedali* could not manage so constant a record, although the activity at the Incurabili was far from negligible. The librettos and records tell us less than we know of Gasparini's activities, but the mainspring of the Incurabili oratorios seems to have been Carlo Pollarolo, whose solidly Venetian roots ensured involvement there until the 1720s. Perhaps it is no surprise that the Mendicanti produced nothing of importance in this line, since Biffi's surviving music suggests that he was a rather orthodox church musician. We might well have expected, on the other hand, some oratorios at the Ospedaletto, given Vinacesi's *Susanna* for Modena. Their absence was probably due to a lack of available talent. There was no singing teacher at the Ospedaletto until 1715 and then he was a 'maestro di solfeggio', a word which implies musicianship rather than singing technique. Both *ospedali* were to make up for their apparent inactivity later in the century.

We know pitifully little of oratorio music from this time. The scores have perished and the librettos are not very informative. Yet what little we can glean hints that there were major developments in the first twenty years of the century and that some of the music may have been of very decent quality. Gasparini's oratorios are an especially sad loss since he was no mean composer, and one surviving oratorio, written after his Pietà period (presumably for Turin[4]), shows him to have been a post-Alessandro Scarlatti figure with a talent for agreeable melody. This is *S. Maria egittiaca*. The title page declares that it is an 'oratorio à 5 voci con violini', but it seems to need only four voices and there is an essential lute part in one aria. The cast is Maria (S), Piacere (A) and Penitenza (T), to whom is added in the second part Lucifero (B). Burney's comment about Gasparini's

---

[3] ASV, Ospedali, Busta 689, notatorio I, fol.34v.

[4] Its source, unrecorded in some reference books, is Turin, Biblioteca Nazionale Universitaria, Ris. mus. II.2. A nineteenth-century hand records that Gasparini 'si diedero nel teatro G. Carignano di Torino alcune opere negli 1718-19'.

Ambleto, given in London as *Hamlet* in 1712, that it bears 'very little resemblance in the conduct of this drama to Shakespeare's tragedy',[5] is not contradicted by the oratorio, which has little dramatic quality. The arias are charming, all the same, being well developed and quite clearly cut off from the recitatives, even though the latter are still in the old 'arioso' manner. Ritornellos are frequent, and obbligatos include not only one for lute, but also others for violin solo and 'violini unisoni'. One aria is marked 'aria pastorale un poco adagio' and is much after Corelli's pastorale, if a little more enterprising harmonically. And there is the grand aria for Lucifer, the usual bass villain complete with low notes and extended fioritura (example 5).

Ex. 5 F. Gasparini: *S. Maria egittiaca*

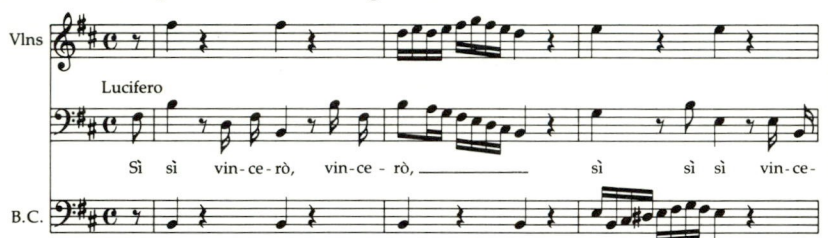

It has to be said that this in no way prepares us for the one surviving score of the Pietà repertory of this period, Vivaldi's *Juditha triumphans* [440], a most remarkable piece by any standards. It was written while Vivaldi was standing in as *maestro di coro* (though he was never so called, or paid as such) after the departure of Gasparini. The governors of the Pietà took over five years to replace Gasparini with Carlo Pietro Grua, and it may be that they were hoping to be able to fill the position with Vivaldi. It was not to be. Vivaldi was a genius; and probably by 1715, after the success of *L'estro armonico*, he knew it. His dealings with the governors were to remain mixed. Sometimes they renewed his contract as *maestro di violino* or *maestro de'concerti* without difficulty; sometimes they did not. Probably their main objection was that he was always going away to produce an opera or give a concert. (The governors at the Mendicanti later had similar difficulties with Galuppi.) We may suspect that, more than

[5] Charles Burney, *A General History of Music*, ed. F. Mercer (London, 1935), p.679.

this, he was a difficult man: he was not called *il prete rosso* for nothing. It might be supposed that having changed the nature of European instrumental music at a stroke with *L'estro armonico* he might have been content to remain a violin virtuoso. Not a bit of it. He really coveted the fame and prosperity which could be found only through the composition of opera.

It is in this light that *Juditha triumphans* must be considered. On the title page it is designated a 'Sacrum Militare Oratorium', to which is added 'hisce belli temporibus'. At the end of the libretto an explanation is added under the heading 'Carmen allegoricum'. The story of Judith venturing into the enemy camp to cut off the head of Israel's enemy Holofernes is interpreted as an analogy with the recènt victory of Venice over the Turks at Petrovaradin. The Venetian triumph was, as it happened, to be short-lived; but that was unknown to the audience in the chapel of the Pietà in 1716. Nor does the effectiveness of the libretto depend on the allegory. It was indeed a little surprising that the story had not been more popular earlier in the history of the oratorio, given the fact that composers were dealing with heroic subjects in opera librettos and that any major composer was likely to find himself writing a serenade to celebrate the military victories of his warring employer. The popularity of the story was in fact to arrive with Metastasio's *Betulia liberata* of around 1730; thereafter it is difficult to avoid it.

Vivaldi had composed a piece not dissimilar for Vicenza in 1713. Its title page tells us almost all we need to know:[6]

LA VITTORIA/ NAVALE/ Predetta dal Santo Pontefice/ PIO V. Ghisilieri/ DELL'ORDINE DE PREDICATORI/ *ORATORIO*/ Da farsi nella Chiesa di Santa Corona/ Di Vicenza. / In occasione dell'Ottavario per la sua/ Cannonizatione solennizato da/ Padri del medesimo Ordine. / POSTO IN MUSICA/ *Dal Signor*/ D. ANTONIO VIVALDI/ Maestro de Concerti del Pio Ospitale/ della Pietà di Venezia. / IN VICENZA, MDCCXIII. / Per Tomaso Lavezari/ *Co Licenza de Superiori*

The note to the reader at the beginning of the libretto tells us that the 'Holy Father Pius V had predicted the victory of the Venetians over the Turks at Lepanto'; so the cast consisted of Pius V, the Angel, Valour and Infidelity. The libretto cannot be said to be very dramatic, if by that action is implied; but as an excuse for highly-charged music it could scarcely be bettered. Here is the Angel, declaiming scarcely Christian sentiments:

> Verserà la turba esangue
> Sopra il mare un mar di sangue
> Dal cadavero infedel.
> Nel svenare, nel punire

[6] Libretto in Venice, Biblioteca Casa di Goldoni.

Un, che degno è di morire
Non fù mai ferro crudel.
Verserà &c.

It is not difficult to imagine that set to music after the manner of Vivaldi's raging motet *Longe mala*. The 'Coro di fedeli' at the end of the first part offers even more obvious opportunities.

Dietro all'orme di duce si grande,
Su, corriamo con rapido piè.
Già n'invitta la tromba, che spande
Somma gloria, e sicura mercè.
Dietro &c.

Infidelity is obviously the stage villain whose opening aria,

La vendetta
Già m'aspetta
A sfogare il mio furor.
Non è incerta
La vittoria
Quando l'ira è col valor.
La vendetta &c.

must surely have been in D major, with large leaps and grand fioritura in the melody. From the libretto it seems that there were about fourteen arias, da capo in form to judge from the repeat marks, and two choruses.

If this presages the manner of *Juditha triumphans*, it remains a surprise how it has been transferred to the world of the music school for girls. Like the Ospedaletto, the Pietà had no singing teacher at this time. Gasparini probably taught the girls, as we may surmise from the governors' praise of him from time to time; and, since he must have been in close contact with the divas of the opera, he probably knew no small amount about their art. It is certainly during his period that the cult of personality began, for we find in his librettos as early as 1706 the names of the ladies who sang, written in presumably by some fans of the performers.[7]

The skill of the orchestra comes as less of a surprise. Vivaldi's tuition on strings must have been excellent. The solo parts of his concertos were written to show off not just his own skills but also those of his pupils. If close examination may reveal which parts he might have played in *L'estro armonico*, the other solo parts are never negligible. The governors of the Pietà had also been moved by Gasparini to appoint wind teachers.[8] If the names of Ertoman or Siber

---

[7] Giancarlo Rostirolla, 'Il periodo Veneziano di Francesco Gasparini', in *Francesco Gasparini (1661-1727): Atti del primo convegno internazionale*, ed. F. Della Seta and F. Piperno (Florence, 1981), pp.85-118.

[8] ASV, Ospedali, Busta 688, notatorio G, fol.174.

mean nothing to us today, we find them turning up quite frequently in the documents of the period, and we may assume that as teachers of 'aboe' (as it is frequently written in the Pietà minutes) they were as good as could be found in Venice. And indeed, it is the variety of woodwind instruments, of dubious and puzzling nomenclature, that has attracted attention in the orchestration of *Juditha triumphans*: there were the salmoè and claren, for example. There is also the question whether women sang the tenor and bass parts in the chorus; this is impossible to settle. It may well be that they did.[9] Certainly, the tenor lines go only to a low d; and that is scarcely out of the range of many of today's contraltos. The bass parts go lower and at times look impossible for women, but they are usually doubled by instruments and could have been fudged without too much difficulty.

We shall probably never know, for the records of the Pietà reveal no payments to priests or singers from St Mark's or lesser churches to fill in the places that no resident at the Pietà could manage. They may have performed gratis, for the care of their souls; they may not have been asked. For the lack of payment to any professional underlines the advantage these girls' schools had. The *figlie di coro* were not professionals in that sense. No arrival by gondola on the day of the performance as at the Fava; no necessity to economise in the hire of rare instruments; no lack of rehearsal time. The music school was complete in itself; the composer was himself a member of the community; and, provided he was content with the talent at his disposal, he had almost perfect conditions to realise even a formidable project like *Juditha triumphans*. We must also remember that 'figlia di coro' did not necessarily imply a young girl. The term included mature teachers who had neither married nor become nuns. Outside the order, they might well have become opera stars.

The other misleading concept is that 'coro' means 'choir' in the modern sense. A nearer meaning would be 'cappella' translated best as 'musical establishment'. There were just fourteen full *figlie di coro* with the privileges of teaching and presumably sharing the proceeds from performances at about this period.[10] The emphasis at the Pietà was perforce on soloists and a well-trained orchestra. It was just right to attract the Lenten crowds.

But the dominant element in *Juditha triumphans* is Vivaldi's genius and personality. From the beginning of his career there can be no mistaking his individual voice. Technically there are some relatively simple explanations. His themes are usually recognisable from their strong rhythms and repeated motifs. These internal repetitions make for easy memorability and for a tight organisation. The faster movements, at least, rarely lack continuous tension. The famed motor rhythms see to that. The other Vivaldian hallmark is the wild purple patch usually involving unexpected harmonies. When we

[9] See Michael Talbot, *Vivaldi* (London, 1978), p.24.
[10] ASV, Ospedali, Busta 688, notatorio G, fols.75v-76.

remember that he came at a time when Corellian orderliness in modulation was sweeping Europe, this is even more surprising.

Juditha triumphans is very Vivaldian; and young Vivaldi at that, for it is an exuberant work, profligate with ideas. The fact that the text is written in Latin should not conceal its essentially operatic nature. We have not, indeed, made a distinction between *oratorio latino* and *oratorio volgare* in these pages, simply because from a musical point of view there is little difference. The rhythms of recitatives are naturally not the same, and the origins of Latin oratorios in concertante church music make for a more arioso style than does setting Italian. But in the arias there is virtually nothing such to remark, especially when it comes to Vivaldi, whose point of reference is in any case instrumental music. Whether the congregations at the Pietà understood Latin very well is unknown, though they had the libretto in hand, and with a knowledge of the story they must surely have been able to follow.

The Latin poetaster (for the Cavalier Cassetti can scarcely be dignified more seriously) has provided a more obviously dramatic text than Metastasio was to do in Italian. For Metastasio, Judith's entry into the enemy camp is best viewed from afar. Cassetti takes us into the very tent of Holofernes and shows us Judith's blandishments. If Alberto Zedda's assertion that there is real characterisation is something of an overstatement, there is no doubt that Cassetti and Vivaldi between them tell the story well. They do not need a *testo*, for the characters between them tell us what is going on: the recitatives are real conversation. The scene between Judith and Holofernes is especially well drawn.

Judith	Non tantus honor
	Tuae famulae donetur.
Holofernes	Tu me honoras.
Jud.	Te colo.
Holo.	Sedeas hic.
Jud.	Non debeo, non.
Holo.	Sic jubeo, et volo.

This is the kind of dialogue one would wish for more frequently in eighteenth-century opera seria. And Vivaldi is surprisingly good, for one so far rather inexperienced, at recitative, finding modulations to change mood or character. His gift of the purple patch comes in especially useful when Holofernes falls in love with Judith (example 6).

Of course it is the arias that most clearly reveal Vivaldi's gifts. All are ample, nearly all are da capo in structure. Several demand virtuoso singing, though this is not a principal preoccupation: when virtuosity becomes display it tends to be given to obbligato instruments. It has to be said that Vivaldi is less good at the lyrical, gentle expression of love than at other things. Where another composer might have set Holofernes' 'Noli o cara te adorantis' as a flowing erotic melody, Vivaldi makes the singer indulge in a rather elaborate

Ex. 6   Vivaldi: *Juditha triumphans*

duet with an oboe; and he even writes out some fioritura for the right hand of the organist, resulting in something nearer to those nineteenth-century *scenas* where sopranos vie with the flute or clarinet in their expression of love. And although the flow is more sustained when Judith speaks of her love for her country in 'Quo cum patriae me ducit amore', one feels that perhaps Gasparini might have done it more convincingly. Nevertheless, in the strong arias Vivaldi has no peer. Holofernes' 'Agitata infido' is rightly said to be one of those 'arie di tempesta' which eighteenth-century composers liked.[11] Vivaldi has exactly the right driving force, direct in diatonic melody, with rhythms emphasising the main beats (example 7).

Vagaus's 'Quamvis ferro' is of much the same kind, more virtuosic in its demands on the singer, its ritornello very like a concerto in its violinistic leaps. His 'Armatae face' is even more in the concerto manner, a vigorous C minor ritornello giving way to the invention of the singer, who is made to perform very violinistic feats with the voice. (It is close to several arias in the solo motets which Vivaldi must have written about this time.) But there is more variety in the arias than might be imagined from this. 'Si fulgida per te' of Abra is a kind of gigue, made less innocent in its middle section by some interesting harmony, while Ozias's 'O sydera, o stellae' opens with a kind of extraordinary French overture, into which the voice is inserted to make dramatic interventions.

In the end, the effect of *Juditha triumphans* is of a large-scale

[11] See the score, ed. Alberto Zedda (Milan, 1971), p.96.

Ex. 7 Ibid.

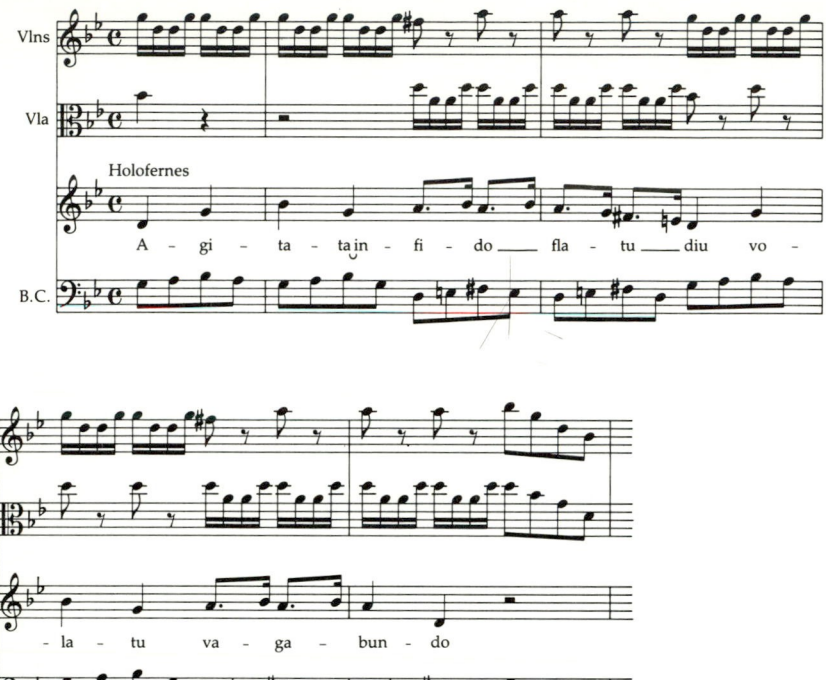

conception, brilliantly carried out. The modest oratorios of the Fava, dating only fifteen years earlier, belong indeed to a different century. This is to be the new world of *opera seria*, great singers, a more than efficient orchestra with some brilliant instrumentalists, and choruses simply written to make a splendid effect, especially at the moment of the *lieto fine*. It makes the *conservatorio–ospedale* the equal of the opera house – though only in music, for such scenic effects as could have been produced in the Pietà must have been limited to drapes; and as we shall see, when later in the century the chapels of the *ospedali* were rebuilt, they offered no opportunity even for that.

This new manner must have come as a great surprise to the audience at the Pietà. As far as we can tell, its rival at the Incurabili was as yet more traditional. Certainly, the librettist Cassetti was known there too. It can be no coincidence that in this same year, 1716, he wrote *Rex regum* [143] for C. F. Pollarolo and that it used a chorus as 'Militae coelestis exercitus' and 'Regni equitalus turbae'; but the *personaggi* revert to the old-fashioned Christmas group of Mary, Joseph and the three Magi, and it is difficult to imagine it a dramatic conception after the manner of *Juditha triumphans*. This is just as true for his *Sterilis faecunda* [358], provided for the younger Antonio Pollarolo at the Ospedaletto in the following year for the day of St Anna who, if the *antefatto* is to be believed, was granted a child after twenty years' sterility by the intervention of an angel. Not the stuff of strong drama, in spite of 'Hostis infernalis' (in the villain-as-bass tradition?). As far as one can tell from the libretto there were eighteen arias, all da capo, and a couple of choruses or ensembles, which implies something on the same scale as Vivaldi, while the cast of seven would not have been beyond the resources of a music school probably less developed than that at the Pietà.

But we are hampered by a lack of scores. The Venetian works of the Pollarolos and Lotti are lacking and the surviving scores to hand must be regarded with some suspicion, since they seem to have been meant for different places and different patrons. C. F. Pollarolo's *Jesabel*,[12] for example, must surely be a work designed not for the Incurabili but rather for Vienna, as its title page's rubric 'con instromenti d'Arco, e da Fiato' suggests. Added to which, if the cast list puts the emphasis on sopranos and contraltos, there is an important part for tenor. Nevertheless, the score is what we might expect from a composer twenty-five years older than Vivaldi, a man who had been part of the Venetian scene in the 1680s and 90s. The arias are da capo, but briefer; there are occasional alternations of aria and recitative, as in an ensemble in the second part which gradually feels itself into the aria in a way of which Monteverdi would not have been ashamed.[13] And if there is an aria for Jesabel 'con trombe', with a stage direction 's'ode in campo la trombe giuliva, che di gloria fa il suol risonar', this is more in the manner of Sartorio than of Vivaldi, who would no doubt have written a mini-concerto movement given such temptation. *Jesabel* is, in fact, an attractive work of the old school; and if Pollarolo produced similar pieces for the Incurabili they should have been grateful.

Two other scores by the elder Pollarolo seem to be of Roman provenance and bow occasionally to Roman tastes.[14] Of the two, *Sansone* may be dated 1706, for a libretto of that year entitled *Samson vindicatus* [139] has survived. We have no news at all of *Saule indemoniato*. The Roman flavour of the latter comes in the trumpet overture and the gigue-like rhythms of several numbers, both features being Corellian (the gigue aria 'Lubra onor contro d'amore' is especially so). But the cast lists in both oratorios put the emphasis on upper voices, and even though they have solo parts for tenor these could be sung by women if necessary, so they might well have been planned originally for the Incurabili. *Saule indemoniato* harks back to the Pallavicino era, with its obbligato trumpet and five-part string textures, the love duet finale and the strophic ritornello arias. The arias in *Sansone* [139] are mainly in the da capo form and are more in

---

[12] Brussels, Conservatoire Royal de Musique, ms M. 1096.

[13] Ibid., fols.86v-92v.

[14] Manchester, Henry Watson Music Library, ms F530 Ps 41 and 44. These surely belong to the 'Jennens' collection. For a discussion of their provenance see Paul Everett, 'Vivaldi Concerto Manuscripts in Manchester: I', *Informazioni e studi Vivaldiani*, v (1984), pp.23-51.

the manner of the 1720s, even to having an 'Affekt', a short figure setting the mood being worked out in detail. It also has some orchestral effects. The use of mutes ('Li violini suonanno con li piombi sopra il scagnello') helps the atmosphere for a love duet between Samson and Delilah 'Vieni dunque ò mio diletto'. There is a genuine *recitativo accompagnato* with held chords for the strings. Both oratorios are obviously operatic, even though the recitatives tend to be monologues rather than conversations. They may tickle the ear; they also have genuine dramatic quality.

The two surviving scores of the period by the other figure associated with the Incurabili, Antonio Lotti, are similarly predictable in style, given what we know of the composer. Both survive in Viennese sources – *L'humiltà coronata* in what seems to be a contemporary copy,[15] the other, *Il voto crudele*, in a nineteenth-century copy taken from an unknown source.[16] Both have librettos by Pietro Pariati, Fux's librettist for that monster entertainment *Costanza e fortezza* of 1723, from which it is logical to deduce that although Lotti's oratorios date from the previous decade, they too must have been meant for the Vienna court.

Between C. F. Pollarolo and Vivaldi in age, Lotti shows in these oratorios a general manner near to that of Gasparini. The modern copyist of *Il voto crudele* has numbered the separate items: there are sixty-six. The arias are not on the whole da capo, usually being marked 'si replica il ritornello'. The melodic style is quite simple, with little fioritura, certainly nothing to compare with Vivaldi. The second part of *Il voto crudele*, where Jephtha, having vowed to sacrifice the first thing he sees, sees his daughter, is indeed operatic: there is a grand recitative for Jephtha and an excellent aria with chorus for the daughter. Schering has little good to say of Pariati's libretto with its 'textlich characterlose Arien',[17] but one cannot help feeling that Lotti was too lyrical a composer to bring out the drama.

Much the same can be said of *L'humiltà coronata*, a more ambitious piece than *Il voto crudele* with longer, often da capo arias, an overture in the style of a concerto grosso, and some chorus work which is integrated into the drama itself. Indeed, in the opening scene the chorus acts as a ritornello with duets and solo sections in between its repetitions. In the second part there is a quite exquisite love duet between Ester and Assuero which shows Lotti's gift for flowing yet direct melody (example 8).

We cannot be sure that these works are representative of Lotti's style for the Incurabili. It is worth noting that although in *L'humiltà coronata* there are only two male voices (against four for soprano and alto), theirs are the most difficult and highly decorated parts, implying the availability of some professionally skilled singers. What

---

[15] Vienna, Österreichische Nationalbibliothek, Cod. 17671.
[16] Ibid., Sammlung Kiesewetter, SA b 8 C4.
[17] Arnold Schering, *Geschichte des Oratoriums* (Leipzig, 1911), pp.202-3.

Ex. 8   Lotti: *L'humiltà coronata*

cannot be in doubt is the languishing of the oratorio in Venice during
the 1720s and 30s. Scarcely a dozen works can be ascribed with
absolute certainty to those years, and even if we may add one or two
more by circumstantial evidence, it scarcely amounts to a flood. This
is rather surprising, since it was precisely at that time that Venice
began to change as an operatic centre from embodying the local style
and manner to become the principal international meeting-place. In
the early 1720s, the composers for the theatres are either natives or
residents: Vivaldi, Pollarolo, Porta, Albinoni. By 1730 there are
notable foreigners: Hasse, Porpora, Vinci. In 1730 the name of
Metastasio enters, and thereafter the stages will be dominated by his
librettos. In the 1720s and 30s the Venetian theatres saw the great
stars – Cuzzoni, Faustina, Bernacchi, Farinelli – at their peak. The
older Venetian opera was dead.

The only native Venetian composer of the period was distinctly
the odd man out: Benedetto Marcello. To call him a 'dilettante' may
be acceptable in the Italian sense of the word, but certainly the
English 'amateur' does not convey his status. He was a skilled and
learned composer. He was not, however, the modern composer of
the 1720s and 30s, making fame and fortune in the theatres; nor had
he need to draw an audience to the *ospedali*. No doubt his noble
friends would have enjoyed the invitation to his palazzo to hear *Il*

pianto e il riso delle quattro stagioni [544] in 1731,[18] written in an archaic style that looks back to the very early years of the century, or *Il trionfo della poesia e della musica* [548][19] – somewhat more up to date, though with Marcello's usual delight in counterpoint and some orchestral effects, which remind us that the piece is on the same subject as Handel's *Ode for St Cecilia's Day*, written in the same decade. This comparison only underlines the fact that while Handel's natural operatic idiom was more likely to draw the crowds to the Theatre Royal in Lincoln's Inn Fields, Marcello's intricate old-fashioned manner was meant for the 'academy', and an academically inclined one at that. This was music of the past, not for the future.

Most of the new foreigners were much too famous to put down roots in Venice. The 250 ducats as *maestro di coro* at the Pietà or Incurabili can have meant little to them. Still less attractive was a post at St Mark's, even though its *maestri* were somewhat better paid. The one man who did settle did so for other reasons: Hasse, who married the Venetian Faustina Bordoni. Not that we know too much about his career in Venice. That he worked for the Incurabili around 1730 is not in doubt, but the surviving documents about that institution are relatively few. We are driven back to the evidence of librettos and word books, of scores which can by various means be ascribed to his Venetian years with some certainty. Fortunately this has been done meticulously in a notable piece of research by Sven Hansell.[20]

It is hard to appreciate the catch of the Incurabili when they acquired Hasse. True, he had not yet become the overwhelming international figure of his middle age; but he was already famous in a way that no Venetian could match. Better still (from the *ospedale*'s point of view), he was au fait with the modern style. Indeed, he *was* the modern style. It was, firstly, a singer's style. In previous operas we find difficult fioritura in the grander arias, be they by Handel or Vivaldi; yet the fioritura comes from the 'Affekt', the meaning, the emotion of the piece. It is an integral part of the music. From Hasse onwards, fioritura is frankly decorative. It is there to show off the singer's skill and nimble throat (as Mozart was to confess in writing *Die Entführung aus dem Serail* half a century later). The triplet figurations so common in Hasse's music are little more expressive than the 'divisions' of sixteenth-century theorists. Which does not, of course, mean that Hasse was not a very capable composer. It suggests more that his work was less dramatic than is desirable for opera – and this may be the reason why there has been no great revival of his work as yet (though lacking a performance on the stage it is impossible to judge an opera, as the Handel revival has shown).

As we have seen, however, oratorio need not be dramatic; and

---

[18] London, British Library, ms Add. 28172.
[19] Brussels, Bibliothèque Royale de Belgique, ms II 3930.
[20] Sven H. Hansell, 'Sacred Music at the Incurabili in Venice at the Time of J. A. Hasse', *Journal of the American Musicological Society*, xxiii (1970), pp.282-301 and 505-21.

here our knowledge of his other music for the Incurabili may offer an indication of its true direction in his hands. For it is plain that he was principally concerned with writing solo motets for the girls and women there. He also set the *Salve regina* in the same manner; and, of course, there was the famous *Miserere*. None of these requires any dramatic gift although it is obvious that, coming from a theatre composer, they may show operatic influence. Hasse, then, was concerned with the liturgical and paraliturgical music of the Incurabili; oratorios were almost incidental.

How this affects his view of the genre may be seen in two scores: *Serpentes in deserto* [148], a work seemingly popular since it survives in several copies,[21] and *S. Petrus et S. Maria Magdalena* [149].[22] Dating them poses its problems. Hansell proposes dates in the early 1730s;[23] and certainly the singers who took part in *Serpentes in deserto* are those who took part in a performance of Porpora's *Sanctus Petrus Urseolus* [150], which can be dated to 1733.[24] But the names are in manuscript, and at least some of the singers seem to have flourished in the period 1745-7; so we cannot be quite sure that they did not sing in a later performance of the Porpora rather than at its première.

No matter; both oratorios are fine works and in spirit surely belong to the 1730s (for the 1740s, as we shall see, seem to have a quite different style and manner). The most noticeable feature is that both are shorter than the traditional oratorio. *Serpentes in deserto* can be divided into eighteen numbers, some extended but not more so than the usual operatic aria. Both pieces are in a single part, not the two 'acts' by now normal; and both end inconclusively. The reason for this is clear. They are to lead into a performance of the *Miserere*. *Magdalena* makes this quite plain:

S. Petrus   Ah tam cito
               Pietas vestra non deserat
               Petrum plorantem
               Mecum fiotite dum orare
               Et de peccato meo dum debeo flere
               Atque dicite meam – Miserere.

This is set as a recitative and concludes with a perfect cadence on G major, from which the *Miserere*, being in C minor, follows on quite naturally. *Serpentes in deserto* ends similarly with a recitative (this time *accompagnato*), and although it does not mention the *Miserere*, what else could 'devoti Davidici concentus' refer to? The general idea is therefore that of the 'introduzione' to the *Miserere* or *Gloria*; Vivaldi

---

[21] We have worked from Vienna, Österreichische Nationalbibliothek, Suppl. Mus. 2110.

[22] Ibid., Suppl. Mus. 0194.

[23] *The New Grove Dictionary*, article 'Hasse', p.281.

[24] Venice, Biblioteca Nazionale Marciana, Misc. 261641.

provided a number of *introduzioni*, but those of Hasse are on a much enlarged scale.

Indeed, everything is on an extended scale. The introductory ritornellos of arias tend to great length (awkward in opera but not here). The opening sections are similarly extended, which means that, with the da capo, the arias themselves are long. As for the demands on the singers, even Vivaldi's fioritura pales a little alongside Hasse's (example 9). These are indeed singers' works. The

Ex. 9 Hasse: *Serpentes in deserto*

recitatives are not perfunctory, but neither are they important, although there are some *accompagnati* of weight. But it is always the arias that have the essential emotional material. The fioritura arias are generally in the heroic manner of opera seria. There are others which are gentler, more sentimental, for Hasse commanded the wide range necessary for opera. The appoggiatura-laden lyrical melody of operas is at times appropriate, as in the duet for Magdalena (example 10).

Ex. 10 Hasse: *S. Petrus et S. Maria Magdalena*

There is a total professionalism in the orchestration, also: although he was content with strings and oboes, Hasse knew when to reinforce phrases and merely to accompany a voice. If the string parts often seem to consist simply of repeated quavers, the ends of phrases see strong unison writing. And, looking at the bowing and expression marks in *Magdalena*, with bowed staccatos and bowed long repeated notes – ♪♪♪♪ – we should do well to remember that, when translated into sound, the conventional repeated quavers may not always have been the same monotonous accompaniment which we see on the page. Yet it is not hard from these scores to see why Hasse was such a great success in his day; these oratorios merit revival, and would be much easier to perform than are the operas, which must probably remain a lost cause.

The other composer who provided the Incurabili with oratorios in the 1730s was probably even better known, though hardly of such talent. Nicolò Porpora was in fact the teacher of some of the great castrati and composed works for their display on the stages of Europe. His career is so full that it must be left to the reference books. As far as Venice is concerned, it may be noted that he seems to have been *maestro* not only at the Incurabili but also, for later periods, at the Pietà and the Ospedaletto. He must have known the ropes very well, having been a pupil at the Naples Conservatorio dei Poveri di Gesù Cristo and subsequently *maestro* at S. Onofrio and the Conservatorio di S. Maria di Loreto. In the 1730s he was much concerned with the Opera of the Nobility in London, where his success contributed to the discomfiture of Handel.

The oratorios he wrote for the Incurabili have not survived in score and we can only cautiously deduce from other pieces[25] what they might have been like. As we would expect, Porpora's oratorios continue the Hasse style in being intended for excellent singers. He seems to have been still less interested in sheer drama even though he was a very experienced opera composer. It is symptomatic that, like Hasse, he wrote a substantial introduction to the *Miserere, Sacrum sumentem lyram* [146],[26] and that pieces from his oratorio *Davide e Bersabea* could be abstracted from the score as independent entities.[27] But whether even in these respects he had as much influence on the Venetian oratorio as Hasse must remain doubtful.

In 1739 it must have seemed that oratorios were to become a rarity in Venice, performed only when a composer had to show off the talents of the pupils at the *ospedali* with something special. Hasse and Porpora were, after all, Europeans rather than Venetians and were certainly not to be expected to put their major energies to such use. But then, that is not very different from the situation at exactly this time in England, where Handel's existing essays in the genre were no less rare. Ten years later all was to seem very different.

---

[25] *Il martirio di S. Eugenia* is a piece clearly written for Naples, and *Il verbo incarne* is a later piece for Dresden.
[26] London, British Library, ms Add. 14127 (autograph).
[27] Cambridge, Fitzwilliam Museum, 2F 23.

3
The Time of Plenty: 1740-1777

Not that we are suggesting any connection between the grand era of Handel's oratorios and the Venetians' revived taste for the genre. It is all too clear a case after the accidental theory of history. Handel's financial failure in opera was one thing; the decision of the Fava to give oratorios again was another. And if there does seem to be some movement towards more interest in musical activities in both the Oratory and the conservatories during the 1740s it hardly adds up to a significant change of heart. There is no Counter-Reformation in sight.

The Fava's re-entry into activity is recorded simply in the fathers' minute book:[1]

1740 3 August. Our musicians having the desire to give oratorios in music, not done since about the year 1700, and the Oratory being capable of doing so at the present, the fathers propose that we agree to their desire which is also that of the fathers; and it was passed 7 votes to 1 with, however, the condition that the sacristy shall be expected to provide only the lighting, and the rest shall be gratis.

Who and how many 'our musicians' were cannot be established. Earlier in the century the Fava had had as *maestro di cappella* Agostino Coletti who had become organist at St Mark's in 1714. They paid an organist for many years and, from information pieced together from various sources, it seems probable that they kept a 'choir' of eight singers for holy days. It was hardly the basis for large-scale performances of oratorios. Nonetheless, away they went.

We know the repertoire exceedingly well, partly from the surviving librettos, now always printed for the congregations; and, even more valuably, from the musical archive of the Fava, in which are preserved many, if not most, of the scores and parts,[2] the latter giving us a detailed idea of how these oratorios were performed. By the standards of the seventeenth century at the Fava, the performances were elaborate; by the standards of churches and courts elsewhere,

[1] Fava Archive, Libro de Decreti I, fol.228.
[2] Paolo Pancino, *Venezia: S. Maria della Consolazione* (Milan, 1969).

they were quite modest. Two desks of first violins, two of seconds, one of violas and an unspecified continuo team, woodwind (generally just oboes) with, more occasionally, horns and/or trumpets: this was the total band. The singers' parts were also generally written out. There was scarcely a chorus (parts marked 'coro' were sung by the soloists). The solo voices varied from just three to, more often, five (occasionally there were also some more minor parts). Sometimes a part for, say, tenor will have been re-written for soprano for a repetition in some later year.

The accounts for these early years of the oratorio revival at the Fava have not been found; but we possess them from the later 1750s[3] and we may draw some tentative conclusions. In the 1740s, the fathers may have paid nobody, for in the 1750s, while they kept up a reasonable expenditure for their festival days (Holy Week, St Philip Neri, the feasts of the Blessed Virgin and so on), we find nothing for Epiphany, their favoured day for oratorios, still less anything marked 'oratorio'. This is surprising. Although the soloists may have given their services, it is harder to imagine the same of the orchestral players, who in Venice had to make their living by such occasional engagements. It seems probable that these expenses were covered in a separate, not yet discovered, account. (The reference to the sacristy in the fathers' minute quoted above means that no expense was to fall on the church account; the Oratory was kept apart for this purpose.) The entries around 1760 which do tell us of the 'oratorios in music' are consolidated payments. When there is an entry, on 13 December 1762, 'for the first oratorio in music', the sum is only 94 lire (about 15 ducats) – which is about the amount one might expect for an orchestra of fifteen.

Where the soloists came from we do not know. The librettos, unlike those of the *ospedali*, do not tell us their names (there was no cult of personality at the Fava); and, although their parts are scarcely virtuoso in the manner of Hasse or Porpora, they require good singers, usually with some experience of recitative. Were they opera singers doing their religious duty? Or were they the better singers at St Mark's? More probably the latter since, as we shall see, the Fava was to have strong links with the basilica in the next thirty years. Indeed, it may be that Coletti was still their *maestro*, in spite of his duties at St Mark's. After all, Giovanni Gabrieli had managed to combine posts at St Mark's and the Scuola Grande di S. Rocco a century and a half earlier; and Venice changed little.

Be that as it may, the fathers of the Oratory managed to put on at least one, sometimes two oratorios each year in the 1740s. There must have been an initial difficulty with repertoire. They could not command Hasse or the like. If Coletti was their *maestro*, he could be called upon. He had, it seems, composed in 1740 *Isaaco, figura del redentore* [46] for the imperial court at Vienna, setting Metastasio, as might be

---

3 ASV, Filippini, Busta 77.

expected. This could be repeated – and was, the year after its composition. Then there was young Galuppi, who had just taken over at the Mendicanti, as a direct result of his oratorio *Sancta Maria Magdalena* [230]. His *S. Maurizio e compagni martiri* [44] was probably given at the Fava in 1740 (we must rely on the word of an antiquary, Piovano).[4] In 1743, the fathers persuaded the singing teacher at the Seminario Ducale, Giorgio Petrodusio, to produce *Il martirio di S. Cecilia* [55]. He wanted to *fare bella figura* and dedicated it to a nobleman, Marcantonio Querini; the fathers were not too keen on that, but graciously permitted it.[5] In general, however, they had to find works from elsewhere.

Luckily, as before, the fathers had many contacts abroad, not least with their famous house at Naples, which seems to have been as active as ever. Nevertheless, it had not greatly cultivated the oratorio as such in recent years; and although the conservatories at Naples were producing composers who were to dominate the European theatres, they too had made no speciality of the genre. Helmut Hucke's judgement that 'the flourishing period of the sacred drama had come to an end with Pergolesi's *Li prodigi della divina grazia nella conversione di S. Guglielmo Duca d'Aquitania* (1731) and Mancini's *Santa Elia profeta* (1733)'[6] may well be accepted.

For although the works of Leo and Feo produced at the Fava in the early 1740s were written in the previous decade, they belong to a retrogressive manner natural to composers brought up many years before. One can see why Leo's *La morte di Abele* [48] and Feo's *S. Francesco di Sales* [45] were given at the Fava in 1741. Neither makes excessive demands on the soloists and, except occasionally in the Feo work, the orchestra is not taxed either. Yet both works have the semblance of music in the later Neapolitan style. The arias are da capo and the recitatives are operatic-type dialogues. Leo in particular likes the Neapolitan triplet figuration and slow-moving harmonies of the time; but he has neither the fire nor the sentimental attractiveness of Hasse. Feo, whose *personaggi* – Heresy, the Angel, S. Francesco and Deceit – look back to the old 'mystery'-type oratorio, is nonetheless more obviously up to date than his colleague setting Metastasio. The *sinfonia*, especially its first movement with fanfare motifs on the trumpets and the string tremolandi, comes straight from the opera house. The arias for Deceit (l'Inganno) are in the oratorio-villain tradition (oddly enough the text of 'Come stridente fulmine' seems very like Metastasio). The ensemble at the end of the first part begins with a recitative that gradually grows into an allegro, which has eventually a da capo. The final quartet is called a 'coro di Cattolici' and belongs to the genre of the *lieto fine*. The whole oratorio is

[4] Francesco Piovano, 'Baldassare Galuppi: note biobibliografiche', *Rivista musicale italiana*, xiii (1906), pp.702ff.
[5] Fava Archive, Libro de Decreti I, fol.234.
[6] *Die Musik in Geschichte und Gegenwart*, IX, col.1325.

vigorous (slow arias are few) and the audience must surely have found it continuously entertaining (one would not presume to say edifying). It was as good a substitute for the moderns at the *ospedali* as could be found.

It cannot be said that the oratorios of less famous composers given at this time reveal a great deal of talent. Chiocchetti's *La circoncisione del santo bambino Gesù* [61] was performed on 1 January 1741. It had the merit of requiring only three singers (the five vocal parts preserved reveal that two had been added for a performance in 1758). The orchestration is simple, with much unison writing for violins. The recitatives are less dialogues than monologues preceding the arias, and the *accompagnato* in the first part consists simply of held notes rather than those changes of figuration and mood which can be so emotional and exciting. Bisso's *S. Atanasio patriarca di Alessandria* [51], performed probably in the following year, is more interesting and ambitious. The tenor role, Arrio sacerdote, is florid and the soprano part, Atanasio, scarcely less so. The orchestral ritornellos to arias are shorter, and indeed the voice sometimes begins. At the end of Part I, there is a real quartet in C minor beginning:

Alessandro	Figlio mio, sempre più bella
Atanasio	Padre, ognor con mio diletto
Alessandro	Trovo in te virtù novella
Atanasio	Scopro in te maggior affetto

Although Bisso has disappeared from the histories and dictionaries of music, he clearly had a flair for operatic music, and this work is in the best traditions of opera seria.

The local boy Petrodusio, composing *Il martirio di S. Cecilia* [55] in 1743, can manage an occasional heroic aria too, but the surviving parts (the score has disappeared) suggest that there were alterations in rehearsal, or at least made by the singers. Even though it was repeated in February 1768 with the famous Venetian tenor and singing teacher Pietro de Mezzo in the role of Almachio, it would be an exaggeration to suggest that the Fava had found a new talent.

Nevertheless, we may suspect that this revival of the genre at the Fava had attracted some attention. We have no means of knowing how many people went to hear these oratorios, but it is significant that the library of the Fava still preserves the copies in bulk of some of the librettos which were presumably printed in the expectation of a congregation. Several survive in literally hundreds of copies – and presumably these were the spares not distributed – which surely indicates an audience to match. And even if these large print-runs were expected to be used at repeat performances, this still confirms the popularity of the 'oratorios in music'.

By the middle of the decade, the *ospedali* were following the example of the Fava more seriously. They had had a few years of uncertainties and staff changes around 1740; five years later most of these had been settled. At the Mendicanti, Galuppi was now in full control and, after his success with *Sancta Maria Magdalena* [230], was producing oratorios. At the Pietà, after an unsatisfactory interlude with Porpora (who left in spite of a much exalted salary), they settled in 1744 on Andrea Bernasconi, who was to become a favourite opera composer at Dresden in the 1750s. The Ospedaletto too had a brief period of Porpora before finding Gaetano Pampani, another substantial opera composer. But the Incurabili managed to secure the best prize (as it seems in retrospect), Nicolò Jommelli, a young Neapolitan whose promise was to be splendidly fulfilled.

Two of the *ospedali* were also involved in building works. At the Pietà a whole new church was begun in 1745, apparently on a much larger scale than the old one in which Vivaldi had performed. We do not know precisely when it came into commission for music and liturgical ceremonies, but it may be significant that it was given two choir galleries and that Bernasconi wrote music which could have used them before he left in 1753. The Mendicanti did not do anything quite as radical, but in February 1744 their governors decided to embark on 'works to enlarge the *cantoria*'.[7] There had been complaints that the members of the choir were crowded together uncomfortably and that they could not see the *maestro* directing the performance.[8] All of which indicates some prosperity and musical health.

The composers at work in this ambience were, almost without exception, opera composers: there is no sign of the old guard at St Mark's, for even Galuppi's active period there was later. Indeed that was the trouble. Galuppi was for ever disappearing to the far ends of Europe, and around 1750 the governors at the Mendicanti were dissatisfied with his efforts. On 27 December 1749 they instructed the two members charged with the supervision of the choir to look into the situation, 'a perceptible diminution of the public in the chapel of the *ospedale* having been noticed on festival days when there is music'.[9] Worse, on 24 February 1750 they reported back with what amounts to a mild motion of censure on Galuppi; and the governors more or less told him to attend to their affairs more diligently.[10] It can hardly have been a coincidence that this was precisely the period when that fruitful collaboration with Goldoni was beginning. 1750 saw *Il mondo alla roversa* at the Teatro S. Cassiano, *Arcifanfano re dei matti* and *Il paese della Cuccagna* at the S. Moisè. This was no light load in itself and must explain why Galuppi was neglecting the Mendicanti. It was a constant problem for the *ospedali*. Nonetheless, about half a dozen oratorios were given each year in Venice (compared with about fifteen operas), which is not a bad record.

---

[7] Giuseppe Ellero, *Arte e musica all'Ospedaletto* (Venice, 1978), p.187.
[8] See Denis Arnold, 'Music at the Mendicanti in the Eighteenth Century', *Music and Letters*, lxv (1984), pp.345-56.
[9] Ellero, op. cit. (n.7), p.188.
[10] Ibid., p.189.

It must not be assumed that because opera composers were so deeply involved all these oratorios were religious operas. The music which Bertoni wrote for the Feast of St Mary Magdalene [242] in 1752 as his first big occasion after taking up Galuppi's post was a series of motets, as the word book ('libretto' seems misleading in this context) shows.

IN FESTO S. MARIAE MAGDALENAE

Modi concinendi a filiabus Xenodochii S. Lazari Mendicantium.
Chori moderatore Ferdinando Bertoni.
Venetiis 1752
Nel Dixit il versetto De Torrente cantato dalla Caliari bresciana.
Versetto a due nel De profundis Fiant aures cantato dalle due Bresciana e
   Bergamasca.
Nel Magnificat il Gloria cantato da D. Santina Guardi bergamasca.
D. Angela Cristinelli la Salve.
Inoltre: Dulci murmure stillate, D. Angela Caliari; De nubiloso coelo frementi,
   D. Justina Garganego; Umbre cadunt, prata rident, D. Beatrice Fabris.

And even when there is some narrative link, the story line may nonetheless be weak. There is not much dramatic excitement to be had in the *Pastorale per la natività di Gesù Cristo* [78] for which Carcani wrote the music heard at the Fava probably in 1750. The cast list consists of an Angel together with Tirsi and Alessi, who presumably provide the pastoral elements. Another festival at the Fava saw a series of 'moral cantatas' [112]: the first on the theme of Jephtha about to sacrifice his daughter; a second, *L'innocenza ricovrata e difesa*, in which the characters are Innocence and the 'sacred spirit of Rome'; the third, a 'sentiment of penitence'; the fourth, a meditation by St Philip; and finally, 'The return of the Soul to God', in which those traditional 'morality' figures, the Angel, the Soul and the Demon, are the protagonists. From the librettos it is clear that these were a series of da capo arias interspersed with recitatives of no great utility. Nor was Metastasio always inclined to drama. A Christmas piece [57] at the Fava in 1744 is of the old 'morality' kind with a 'Genio celeste' giving the introduction, the *personaggi* being Faith, Hope and Divine Love.

Nevertheless, one cannot help feeling that it was Metastasio who gave impetus to the movement towards what one might call the 'oratorio seria', an offshoot of the opera seria. The verse of *La morte di Abele* [48], set by Leo, is in Metastasio's best style. Admittedly there is no *lieto fine*, and he points out the moral of the story as a good *abate* should.

Parla l'estinto Abele: con le chiare
Voci del sangue il parricida accusa.
Mortali, a noi si parla. Ogn'un di noi
Ha parte nel delitto,
Ma non l'ha nel dolor. Detesta ogn'uno

Le vie degli empi, e v'introduce il piede;
Abborrisce Caino, e in se nol vede.

His *Il Giuseppe riconosciuto* [95], set by Hasse and given at the Fava at some unspecified period, is even more in the manner of opera seria, not only complete with *lieto fine* but also including comparable arias:

D'ogni pianta palesa l'aspetto
Il difetto, che'l tronco nasconde,
Per le fronde dal frutto, o dal fior.
Tal d'un'alma l'affanno sepolto
Si travvede in un riso fallace:
Che la pace mal finge nel volto,
Chi si sente la guerra nel cor.

Moreover, not only do we have the manner of opera seria: we have its characters. We have Thanete, that well-known archetypal confidant of Joseph; and Joseph's wife Asenetha, not much known to readers of the Old Testament but here someone of not inconsiderable importance who, indeed, sings the final aria. Metastasio sometimes adopts a scholarly tone. In *Gioas re di Giuda* [82] he begins with an 'argomento' which looks even more like an opera seria and a list of very unbiblical *personaggi* attached as source list to his story, from IV *Kings* (= II *Kings* in Authorised Version) xi–xii and II *Paral* (= II *Chronicles*) xxii–xxiv.

Such departures from Holy Writ may not have disturbed Metastasio, poet to the Holy Roman Emperor at Vienna. Lesser men, under more detailed scrutiny by local censors, showed more concern. The anonymous author of *L'innocenza rispettata* [104], given at the Fava in 1765, the libretto produced 'con Licenza de' Superiori', was moved to 'protest that the author, having moved a little in the present *componimento* from the Holy Story, has done so only to express the same with greater facility, [and] professes to be a true Catholic'. His cast list does not inspire much confidence from this point of view:

Amramo, father ⎫
Giacobbeda, mother ⎬ to Gioachino, later called Moses
Maria, sister ⎭
Eliezer, confidant of Amramo
Chorus of Egyptian soldiers

The action, we are told, takes place in 'Jerusalem, inside and outside the temple of Solomon'. Similarly the author of *Salomone re d'Israele* [80], whose cast list is of somewhat more respectable ancestry, tells us that his source is III *Kings* (= I *Kings*) i. 'Argomenti' are, in fact, commonplace in librettos of this period and seem remarkably like the *antefatti* of opera books. Certainly the old days of narrators and biblical tracts have gone.

The 1740s, it must be remembered, were the last years of the domination of opera seria. The 1750s saw the change to the more sophisticated opera buffa of Galuppi and Goldoni, although it did not kill off opera seria for two or three decades yet. The language and the manner of opera seria, which were not in any way unfortunate for oratorio, came naturally to the librettists in the wake of Metastasio and the composers in the wake of Hasse. Indeed the opera seria formula was more suited to oratorio than to the theatre. Those modern objections to opera seria do not apply. There can be no 'exit' convention; the vanity of singers need not be taken so seriously; the complications of the opera plots are much reduced, partly by the nature of the subject, partly by the fact that the two-part oratorio is perforce simpler than the three-act opera. The usual complaint that there is no development of the characters becomes irrelevant when the main raison d'être becomes a religious lesson. At the same time, the issues are essentially about great men and women – as in opera seria – and the grand manner thus entirely appropriate.

Perhaps it is not surprising that the genre proved happy even for minor composers: certainly the standard of oratorios surviving today at the Fava is higher than one might imagine from the names of the *maestri*. Most prove capable of a Neapolitan-style opera overture, usually in three movements, the second (decorative) and third (dance-like 3/8) perhaps of no great weight, but the first often quite heavily scored (Scalabrini's *Il Giuseppe riconosciuto* [76], for example, employing *trombe da caccia*) and portending great issues. The arias are da capo or dal segno (omitting the first ritornello) in form and are usually extended pieces which allow the emotion to develop. It is natural that oratorios given at the Fava should have relatively little fioritura to tax the singers; but when difficult arias were deemed necessary for the expression of heroic feeling, composers were not hesitant to write them. In Corbisiero's *Gioas re di Giuda* [82], the soprano embarks on just such an aria as would offer even great opera singers a challenge (example 11). Such arias were quite often scored

Ex. 11   Corbisiero: *Gioas re di Giuda*

heavily, with horns and oboes, though admittedly the skilful professional composers have the knack of lightening the sonority while the voice is singing and using the additional instruments in the ritornellos or short interludes between phrases. The more lyrical arias are basically scored with strings alone; and the direct, tuneful style of melody must have been more suitable for the modest (as we must assume) singers at the Fava. (See example 12.)

Ex. 12 Bisso: *Assalone*

Violins double the voice

But often the most interesting numbers are the *recitativi accompagnati* which became more important as the 1740s and 50s went on. The advantage of the *accompagnato* is that its use of the orchestra gives it emotional weight, while the fact that it does not repeat words (except for emphasis) means that it can change mood rapidly and decisively. Some examples are extended pieces, usually for a single character – though dialogue *accompagnati* are not unknown – at a moment of crisis. A favourite place in the oratorio for them is near the end of the second part, just before the dénouement, but the more skilful composers often have three or four of them and may put one quite early to raise the emotional temperature. Scalabrini, at the moment where Giuda is in despair at the prospect of never seeing his brother again, involves the orchestra in a delicate negotiation of distant keys (example 13).

The master of all these means to appear in Venice in the 1740s was Nicolò Jommelli, who while still a young man became *maestro di coro* at the Incurabili. Although he stayed in Venice only briefly and at a time when it can hardly have been imagined that he would become a major opera composer, there is no doubt that he served the Incurabili well, for some of his solo motets for the women are as fine samples of the genre as can be found; added to which was an oratorio which can be accounted at least a near masterpiece, *Betulia liberata* [*96*].

Metastasio's libretto has had a bad press from Alfred Einstein, who describes one of the 'comparison' arias as 'this nonsense' and points out that the attention of the audience is not held mainly by Judith or Holofernes, as presumably it should be: 'For him [Metastasio] the important theme was the conversion of an Ammonite prince, Achior, who, badly treated by Holofernes, goes over to the Jews, discusses religious questions with Ozia, the *Principe* of the besieged

Ex. 13   Scalabrini: *Il Giuseppe riconosciuto*

Ex. 13 cont.

di - ce   e   tor - na ad ab - brac - ciar - lo.   O - ra   di   nuo - vo

city, and is moved only by Judith's deed to give up his heathen scepticism'.[11] But Einstein has fallen into his own trap, for he has already pointed out that an oratorio is not an opera. That Mozart apparently set it in terms of opera seria – and an opera seria which has already lost much of its original spirit – does not negate this maxim. In fact, Mozart was writing in the 1770s when, as we shall see, the influence of opera buffa was already marked and the Metastasian libretto, meant for the da capo aria and the heroic castrati, could not be satisfactorily adapted. In any case, it is not difficult to see why Metastasio was so popular that his *Betulia liberata* was set, by all kinds of composers, a score or more times. He was, after all, a genuine poet, a fact which quickly emerges from comparison with the Venetian poetasters of other oratorios. Then he had the happy knack of encapsulating an emotion or *affetto* in words with concrete images which allow the musician to 'paint' them and thus bring them to life. If the emotions tend to be exalted rather than domestic, in oratorio this is a positive advantage.

Jommelli certainly found it so. The first aria, sung by Ozia, Prince of the besieged Bethulia, may not take us directly into the dramatic action. It certainly gives the sense of a ruler encouraging his people, as even the English translator for a London performance of 1763 manages to convey.[12]

D'ogni colpa la colpa maggiore	Of all the faults, the greatest sure
E l'eccesso d'un'empio timore	Is an unhallow'd fear,
Oltraggioso all'eterna pietà.	Injurious to th'eternal Goodness.

[11] Alfred Einstein, *Mozart: his Character, his Work* (London, 1946), pp.387f.

[12] The/ Deliverance of Bethulia:/ an/ Oratorio,/ of/ Signor Metastasio's,/ Set to Music by/ Signor Jomelli,/ as performed at/ His Majesty's Theatre in the Haymarket,/ for the Benefit of/ Signor Guarducci,/ Musician to his Royal Highness the/ Great Duke of Tuscany,/ on the 25th of February, 1763.

Chi dispera non ama, non crede:	Those who despair, nor love, nor yet believe;
Che la fede, l'amore, la speme	Faith, love, and hope, three torches, are combin'd,
Son tre faci, che splendono insieme,	Not one of which gives light without the other.
Ne una ha luce, se l'altra non l'ha.	

Even the fifteen-year-old Mozart rises to this, but the idiom of 1770 tends to the sentimental rather than the heroic. Jommelli, on the other hand, writes in a manner suitable for a back-against-the-wall leader, beginning with a massive ritornello tightly developed from two short motifs. (See example 14.) In both these settings, there is some taxing fioritura. Indeed, Mozart's heroics rely on it. Jommelli is more interested in the lie of the tessitura, especially the lower reaches of the alto voice which can be contrasted with the upper notes.

Ex. 14

a Jommelli: *Betulia liberata*

b Mozart: *La Betulia liberata*

Among the sixteen da capo arias a few are more gentle in *affetto*. Jommelli's music, however, is rarely relaxed. He usually works in short phrases, based on strong rhythms, which may be expanded as the aria proceeds but are never loose.

He is also a master of the *accompagnato*, which he sees as a means to gain dramatic pace. When Judith returns victorious having cut off Holofernes' head, she has to narrate her adventures (it could hardly have been shown directly even in opera seria). A secco recitative must surely be too flat for such a story; an aria could scarcely convey the action; so an *accompagnato* is the chosen medium. There are no less than twenty lines of Metastasio to set. Jommelli begins quietly in secco recitative; paints the sleeping camp with muted strings; shows the increasing excitement in held chords; develops a little motif as the climax approaches; takes the mutes off for the moment of Holofernes' death; and finishes with some military dotted rhythms as Judith celebrates her triumph. It seems at the end a famous victory indeed.

There is little for the chorus to do throughout the oratorio. When it is employed, it is used imaginatively, Ozia's 'Pietà, se irato sei' being punctuated by discreet *sotto voce* phrases; and in one recitative the chorus shouts off stage to help the atmosphere of siege. In the last number in Part II it sings a brief piece, in Neapolitan *stile antico* counterpoint, which is brought back several times, creating the effect of a true finale. Metastasio has built this treatment into his libretto, and a comparison of Jommelli and Mozart shows very clearly the difference twenty-five years had made in musical style. Mozart, used to the sectional opera buffa finale, writes an extended multi-sectional piece. Jommelli sticks together a chorus, an aria, a passage of what for want of a better term may be called accompanied recitative (it is so melodious that it seems almost to be an aria) and a duet. The opera reformer-to-be is already at work.

Jommelli was still a young man when he wrote *Betulia liberata* [*96*]. He had, admittedly, composed half a dozen operas for the Venetian theatres and was an up-and-coming star worth watching. The oratorio was part of this progress, for it clearly was widely diffused, several scores still surviving in different parts of Europe, including one which may have been used for Guarducci's benefit in London.[13]

It seems that *Betulia liberata* was first given at the Philippine Oratory at Genoa in 1743, and that only later did it arrive in Venice, where it emerged at the Fava. Nonetheless it is in the heroic tradition going back to Vivaldi's *Juditha triumphans* [440] and, although by a Neapolitan, is not Neapolitan in spirit; which fact may be tested by a comparison with Jommelli's other famous oratorio, *La passione di Gesù Cristo* [74], composed in 1749 for Rome or Naples, given at the Fava in Venice at an unknown date.[14] The libretto is again by Metastasio who has reduced the *personaggi* to just four, S. Maria Maddalena, S. Giovanni, S. Pietro and Giuseppe d'Arimatea, with a chorus of 'Seguaci di Gesù'. Obviously, the heroic opera seria manner of *Betulia liberata* will not do, even though the means – da capo arias and *accompagnati* – are much the same, with the chorus playing a somewhat larger part. To call it 'sentimental' is in no way to use the term in a pejorative sense. It is 'sentimental' in the way of much eighteenth-century religious painting. It is certainly not 'baroque', as a comparison with Bach's passions makes quickly evident. Here is no juxtaposition of disparate elements – arias, *accompagnati*, choruses and chorales. The language is opera seria. Nor is Jommelli an anguished Protestant, fearful of death and damnation. He is secure in his faith and salvation. There are some fine things, not least the overture with its mixture of slow and fast in the opening movement in a manner we today associate with 'classical' Gluck. The *accompagnati* are many, and their changes of mood are brought about by varied thematic material. The end of the first part even brings this to the chorus which, after some solid Neapolitan counterpoint, ends in a quasi-recitative manner and, so it feels, on the dominant (example 15).

Given music as fine as this, it is a pity that the Protestant Passion has driven out the 'passion-oratorio'; Jommelli's manner may not be as strong as that of Bach, but it certainly offers a valid alternative. Nor can it be criticised as being hindered by the dead conventions of opera seria. It is noticeable how the pattern of aria–recitative–aria is breaking down. There are larger-scale considerations. The first chorus, for example, is the usual contrapuntal affair; but it leads directly into a duet between Maddalena and Giovanni which in turn ends with a short passage of *accompagnato* before the chorus is recapitulated – and it ends not with the normal firm ending, but with a pianissimo whisper 'umanità'.

---

[13] It was also performed in Ravenna in 1759, which year was 'the centenary of the translation of the Beata Vergine del Sudore to which a new altar was solemnly dedicated'. The orchestra was much the same in numbers as at the Fava. See Paolo Fabbri, *Tre secoli di musica a Ravenna* (Ravenna, 1983), p.80.

[14] The score and parts preserved at the Fava offer no clue. The score in the Biblioteca Nazionale Marciana, It. IV. 565 [=9845], was acquired by that library in 1889.

Ex. 15 Jommelli: *La passione di Gesù Cristo*

Not that such intermingling of numbers is entirely unknown elsewhere in oratorio of this time. There are several examples of a mixture of *secco* and *accompagnato* recitative; choruses often enough have short solo sections. If the arias tend to be more conventional in general plan, they too can contain the unexpected. An aria for l'Anima in the anonymous *L'impenitente peccatore* [43], which from its style seems to belong to the early phase of the Fava revival, begins with a gesture from the voice which the orchestra takes up, largo, before embarking on the main matter (example 16). In Scalabrini's *Il Giuseppe riconosciuto* [49], second sections of da capo arias are sometimes in strong contrast with the first section. In all, we must avoid assuming that there is a stereotype, even in this Neapolitan-style oratorio, with its links to the opera seria.

It is in a native Venetian, however, that we see the beginnings of something stylistically new. Galuppi, it may be remembered, was at the beginning of the renewal of enthusiasm for the oratorio at the Mendicanti in 1740. He did not immediately continue his efforts in the genre, and when we consider the obvious success of *Sancta Maria Magdalena* [230] we can understand the annoyance of the governors at his departure for London. However, when he eventually did return, he resumed his work for the Mendicanti. *Isaac* [232] (1745), *Judith* [233]

Ex. 16 anon.: *L'impenitente peccatore*

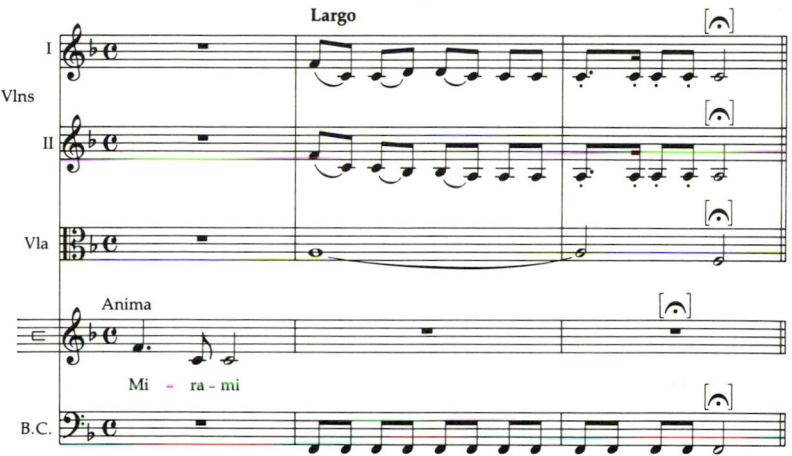

(1746) and *Jahel* [235] (1747), with the *Rhythmi sacri* [236], *Devoti affectus* [237] and *Devoti sacri* [238], witness to his efforts during those years. He also wrote *Adamo caduto* [69] (1748; in the score I-Tn Foà 51 known as *Adamo ed Eva*) for the Fava; and although the scores of only *Adamo* and *Jahel* survive, we can perhaps see why the governors of the Mendicanti could complain of lack of audiences, and hence of funds proceeding from the performances. With the exception of *Judith* (which does not set the by now usual libretto of Metastasio) the heroic manner of the Neapolitans is absent in subject matter and, if the score of *Adamo* is typical, in musical manner also.

The qualification 'if the score is typical' is a necessary caution because in fact there are clearly two oratorios by Galuppi on the theme, one [69] dating from his Mendicanti years, the other [194] written for the Incurabili in the 1770s. There are a number of scores of the former extant, and until comparisons have been made between them, we cannot be sure exactly what the source material at our disposal represents; but the score surviving in the Marciana[15] seems likely to belong to his Mendicanti period. The cast list is as follows:

Angelo di Misericordia	Soprano
Eva	Soprano
Angelo di Giustizia	Alto
Adamo	Tenor

This has the look of an old-fashioned mystery oratorio: there is certainly no sign of the modern 'heroic' manner in it, though in practice Galuppi's experience of opera seria is not lacking. The arias are nearly all 'dal segno', and several have 'cadenza' spots. The music for the angels tends to the heroic way, with coloratura, *messa di voce* effects, use of high registers and the like. Sometimes there is a full

---

[15] Venice, Biblioteca Nazionale Marciana, It. IV. 1021 [=10794].

orchestral accompaniment with violin scales and strong unison writing. But it is noticeable that the parts for Adam and Eve are often more domestic and *buffo* in style. This cannot be ascribed to a conscious superhuman–human division: the two manners overlap, with Adam's first recitative and aria, for example, distinctly *seria*; and one aria for the Angelo di Giustizia is a gentle 3/4 andante which would not come amiss in an opera buffa. Nonetheless, the new 'sentimental' *buffo* melody, with its shorter phrases and more direct tunefulness, is often enough in evidence. The three-movement overture has the lighter touch as does the final 'chorus', a quartet in 3/8 which is more opera buffa than *lieto fine*.

The change in tone is hardly surprising. If Galuppi had spent the 1730s writing opera seria (and setting a great deal of Metastasio) for Venice, Turin, London – indeed, anywhere that gave him a commission – from about 1745, the opera giocosa was becoming more and more clearly his métier. *La forza d'amore* and *L'ambizione delusa* in 1745, *Il protettore alla moda* (1747), *L'Arcadia in Brenta*, *Il conte Caramella* and *Arcifanfano re dei matti*, all in 1749, show the way it was to be. 1750 saw the die cast with *Il mondo della luna*, the Goldoni collaboration thereafter firm.

One would not wish it otherwise, given the future greatness of opera buffa, due much to these two collaborators, as fit for each other as Gilbert and Sullivan. Even so, another score surviving from this period shows that Galuppi's gift in oratorio is not to be despised. It seems that *Il sagrificio di Jefte* [92] was commissioned from Florence in 1749: it arrived at the Fava only seven years later. It is certainly not a conservatory piece, the small cast with its emphasis on the father figure of Jephtha, and the lack of brilliance in manner, being much more in the tradition of the Oratory. The plot is, of course, the classic Old Testament story of the sacrifice of Jephtha's daughter in answer to a cruel vow – the story that had stimulated Carissimi to a masterpiece almost a century earlier. But whereas Carissimi had taken the opportunity to finish with a great elegiac choral scena, Galuppi's librettist turns it into opera seria, complete with *lieto fine*. The dénouement is done quite skilfully. Rebecca cannot believe that a sign from heaven has saved her daughter: 'E come? ah tu deridi/ Il mio misero duol', and it takes the rest of the cast to reassure her. In the end there is the customary chorus in praise of 'Santa Religione' (although the chorus seems to have had little to do before this miracle). Human sacrifices were not to eighteenth-century taste.

Galuppi's music is essentially more serious than that of *Adamo ed Eva* [69] even though, at first sight, the forms and manner seem much the same. The overture, for example, looks like a three-movement *buffa* sinfonia, a D major allegro followed by a *galant* andante and the usual 3/8 dance to end. Closer examination reveals a sophisticated sonata first movement, with a passage after the double bar which may not develop the material in Haydn's manner but nonetheless provides serious changes of key and some unexpected harmonies.

The andante does not go into the facile triplets of many such movements and is similarly surprising harmonically. Only the finale seems lightweight for the serious matter to come.

In the opening recitative it is clear that the scale is larger than usual. This is no simple telling of what is, after all, a quite straightforward story; it involves a great deal of comment on life and religion. For modern taste this seems excessive, but the scale of the arias matches it and perhaps it is necessary in the cause of balance. The arias are mostly 'dal segno', the ritornellos being so ample that a cut before the reprise is desirable. In style, some are 'buffo sentimental', others distinctly *seria*. The difference is largely a matter of ornamentation. The 'sentimental' melody is full of small-scale ornaments repeated a number of times either within the phrase itself or within the opening paragraph. Sefa's aria 'Se per me serbi in petto' (example 17) is a good example of the style, the relatively slow harmonic rhythm allowing the trills and twirls to be displayed.

Ex. 17   Galuppi: *Il sagrificio di Jefte*

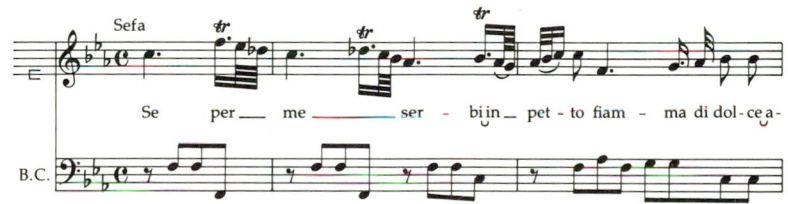

From this, one can see why the singing teacher at the Mendicanti was called the 'maestro di maniera'. It requires a particular skill to perform such neat ornaments (as opposed to the breath control and power needed for the old heroic style), and the shaping of line from this kind of detail presents difficulties. The *seria* arias are more direct in melody, ornaments taking the form of fioritura in the older style; the phrases are more extended and often the orchestra is given an important role. Not all of them are heroic or even solemn. Jephtha's 'Straggi minaccia il cielo' in the first part is in essence a gigue, not unlike those of Handel (and its wit is not altogether in place here). At the climax of the second part, Jephtha's departure from Rebecca, there is a fine *accompagnato*, full of changes of mood (and hence of musical material), succeeded by an aria in the grand manner, the voice part plain and sustained, the orchestra providing both themes and atmosphere, with the staccato wind and pizzicato lower strings (see example 18). In the middle section forte-piano indications against

Ex. 18 Ibid.

the constant use of the singer's upper register continue the mood.

In spite of this and a number of other arias in similar vein, it has to be said that Galuppi has moved away from the heroic style of Jommelli and the Neapolitan opera composers. True, there is the *lieto fine*; true, there is a hint of Metastasian imagery in the verse; true, Galuppi is a master of the large-scale aria; yet the final impression is that oratorio is moving not so much towards the *buffo* (for there is no concerted finale, patter songs or even very fast-moving secco recitative) as towards the more delicate pastel shades of emotion. *Il sagrificio di Jefte* is certainly a good oratorio, its music worthy indeed of revival; equally certainly, it represents a change of taste.

Not that Galuppi was, in any case, the man who would carve the change. When he left the Mendicanti in 1751, he became so busy in the theatres that, apart from *Gerusalemme convertita* for Rome to a text by Zeno in 1752, he wrote no more oratorios until he became *maestro di coro* at the Incurabili a decade later. There were, however, others to take his place. At the Mendicanti, his pupil (or at least disciple) Bertoni took on the job. He was exactly what the governors needed, an active young man who would soon make his way in the theatre and was likely meanwhile to devote himself to their service. He did. At the Pietà, Bernasconi was equally energetic; when he left, the Neapolitan Latilla was a good substitute. Gaetano Pampani at the Ospedaletto was in the same mould, not a native Venetian but interested enough in the opera houses to stay there and produce religious music for the *ospedale*. Even the Fava had put its house in order. Coletti, who had looked after its music for many years, died in 1752 and was succeeded by Saratelli,[16] *maestro di cappella* at St Mark's, no less. On Saratelli's death in 1762, Bertoni, by now organist at St Mark's as well as director at the Mendicanti, took on this further burden[17] – probably not as onerous as it sounds, since the fathers had already an agreement with eight singers, some at least from St Mark's, so that Bertoni probably brought with him friends and already well-rehearsed music.

By this time the fathers were spending a goodly sum on music each year. In 1748 they were paying their singers a total of 180 ducats a year.[18] In 1753 Saratelli's honorarium was 310 lire (50 ducats).[19] In addition there were special payments for various saints' days, Holy Week and so on. These payments do not specify oratorios, but in 1754 the following entry appears in the accounts:[20]

31 March as a supplementary [payment] for the oratorio in music   32 lire

The following year it was 70 lire; 1756, 61 lire 15 piccoli. By 1760 the sum was up to 147 lire 10 piccoli and in 1762 no less than 364 lire.[21] For this latter year, they had three oratorios.[22] There are also sundry payments to copyists, and perhaps for printing librettos, which may apply to these performances. The implication of 'supplementary' in the accounts seems to be that they employed both their regular musicians and others. Again the parts surviving in the Fava library indicate a small band of fifteen to twenty players and very occasionally the use of a chorus: soloists are never more than half a dozen, and are usually four in number. At the *ospedali*, the cast list is on the whole somewhat more numerous, six being normal and seven or eight not unknown.

[16] ASV, Filippini, Busta 76, fols.238v and 364.
[17] Ibid., Busta 77, fol.232.
[18] Ibid., Busta 76, fol.91v.
[19] Ibid., fol.238v.
[20] Ibid., fol.242v.
[21] Ibid., Busta 77, fol.238.
[22] Ibid., fol.230v.

The cult of personality is now high: the names of the performers at the conservatories (though never at the Fava) are always given in the librettos. From these names it is clear that, so far from being young girls, the soloists were by the 1760s often mature women, sometimes of considerable experience. Whereas in the 1740s the names recur for a year or two and then disappear, the singers who first appear around 1748 may be found nearly twenty years later. Fiorina [Florena] Vendramin (of the noble family, presumably) appeared first at the Ospedaletto in 1750 and was still appearing in 1766; the same applies to Beatrix Fabris of the Mendicanti. Santina Guardi and Angela Caliari, both of the Mendicanti, enter the lists in 1752 and were performing in 1769. Cornelia of the Pietà started her career in 1751 and was still taking part in oratorios in 1768, though it was less common for the singers at the Pietà to have such extended careers at this period. It may be that Burney in 1770 was right in finding the standards there lower than those at the other *ospedali*.[23] In any case, the assumption must be that some of these singers were every bit as good as those heard in the opera house, since the women at the *ospedali* were not allowed to leave unless they had found a husband or an agreeable nunnery.

As ever, we lack the scores for the performances at the *ospedali*; but bearing the above in mind, it may not be unfair to consider Bernasconi's *La Betulia liberata* – written, judging by the cast, for Vienna around 1754 – as near the style heard at the Pietà in the early 1750s. Amithal was written for tenor, but the rest of the cast was of upper voices: Ozia a castrato; Charmi 'capo del popolo' for soprano (the Vienna score[24] names Francesca Gabrielli for the performance); while Giuditta herself was taken by no less a figure than Caterina Gabrielli, one of the most famous of all European opera stars. It may also be significant that the chorus is disposed 'alla destra' and 'alla sinistra' at one point: if the new chapel was in use by this time, that is exactly what we would expect at the Pietà with its two choir galleries.

The general manner is not far from Jommelli's a decade earlier. This is opera seria. The arias are generally 'dal segno' which, considering the usual length of the ritornellos, is not surprising.There is the heroic stance in the arias, for Giuditta especially, conveyed not so much by fioritura as by brilliant high writing; and the fioritura itself is in the style of Jommelli rather than of Galuppi (example 19). The harmonies are simpler, slower-moving and more predictable than Jommelli's; and indeed the manner is tending towards the classical and away from the baroque. It may be only by hindsight that the 'French' connection with Parma (where Bernasconi spent some earlier years) seems significant; nevertheless, this was not the general direction being taken by Italian music. The orchestration is distinctly

[23] Charles Burney, *Music, Men and Manners in France and Italy 1770*, ed. H. Edmund Poole (London, 1969), p.78.

[24] Vienna, Österreichische Nationalbibliothek, Cod. 17085.

Ex. 19 Bernasconi: *La Betulia liberata*

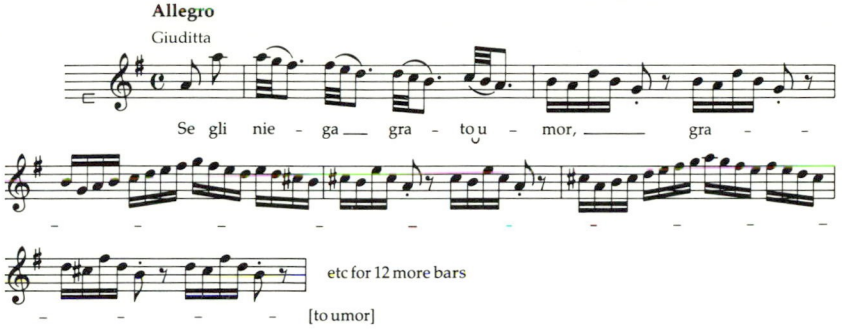

more mature than in most oratorios of the time; there is even a written-out timpani part in the first chorus. The overture is in the usual three-movement pattern, the first one rather weighty and symphonic. Bernasconi's operatic talents are everywhere, especially in the *accompagnati*, grand scena-like pieces for a single person, full of abrupt changes of mood and tone. This is an excellent score and makes us understand why he was so highly valued in Munich. The Pietà was fortunate to keep him for nearly a decade.

Beside this brilliance, Bertoni's efforts – at least those surviving in score at the Fava – may seem a little lack-lustre. But in some ways they are more forward-looking. We must not jump to the conclusion that because he held church posts in Venice for virtually the whole of his professional life he was either ecclesiastical in approach or just a provincial: Galuppi's career was very similar. Bertoni's forty-nine operas were given not just in Venice, but also in London, Genoa, Turin and Rome. The fact that he set Calzabigi's *Orfeo ed Euridice* shows the breadth of his tastes. (Most Italian opera composers would scarcely have heard of Gluck and would not have known what to make of his 'classical' style if they had!) If he was not a man who had that passion for the theatre which is evident in great opera composers, he was well aware of the necessities of dramatic music; and it is significant that at a time when opera buffa was sweeping the stages, he was on the whole commissioned to write opera seria, Zeno and Metastasio texts occurring frequently. A man who could write an *Ifigenia in Aulide* for Turin must surely be just the composer for oratorios. No wonder the Archbishop of Salzburg was interested in him as a possible Kapellmeister in 1778. Nevertheless, one cannot help feeling that it was music rather than dramatic feeling which was his strong point. Some of his church music is excellent, not least three settings of the *Miserere*;[25] and when we look at the librettos printed for the festivals at the Mendicanti, his works are often called 'modulamina sacra' and turn out to be a series of motets written specifically for his various singers. He also wrote a quantity of instrumental music: he was after all an organist.

[25] Arnold, op. cit. (n.8), pp.352f.

If, therefore, Bertoni cannot be considered to possess the genius of his master Galuppi, it remains true that his surviving oratorios are by no means uninteresting. They were admittedly written relatively early in his long life and are for the Fava. *Il ritorno del figliuol prodigo* *[68]*,[26] dating from 1747, is the most conventional of them, being a string of dal segno or da capo arias interspersed with extended dialogue in recitative. There is a duet and two 'cori' (clearly meant for the soloists) but no grand *accompagnato* such as Galuppi and Jommelli were writing about this period. The overture is in the usual three movements and of no great power either. It may be that Bertoni was being cautious about the forces at the Fava, for the orchestration is rarely adventurous, and the soprano parts are rarely taxing. (Was the prodigal son taken by a boy, one might even ask?) The alto part is more demanding and the tenor most of all – though singers from St Mark's could have managed them. The attractive feature of the score is Bertoni's directness of melody and rhythm. When there is fioritura it tends to reinforce the accentuation: there is no hint of that charming frivolity to be found in Galuppi. Here, for example, is an aria in which the father is angry (as well he might be) with the prodigal son. The military rhythms and the syllabic melody are reinforced by the large leaps; the words are in the best Metastasian manner (example 20).

Ex. 20   Bertoni: *Il ritorno del figliuol prodigo*

[26] Venice, Biblioteca Nazionale Marciana, It. IV. 1093 [=10880], has parts as well as a score, and seems to have been part of the Fava collection.

Four years later Bertoni is both more experienced and more ambitious. Of course *Davidde trionfante di Golia* [79] is a more promising subject, with a fine dramatic climax; but Bertoni takes full advantage of it in a way that *Il ritorno del figliuol prodigo* does not suggest possible. The scale seems distinctly larger, even if there is not much difference in actual size. The orchestra is larger, demanding flutes and oboes, horns and trumpets; and the bassoon part is at times written out, not just part of the continuo-bass team. In the Fava score there is no overture; but this is clearly a working copy, made either at composition or at rehearsal stage, and it is more than possible that an overture was added later. Certainly its absence is no reflection on the capabilities of the orchestra which is engaged skilfully and committedly in the arias. The splendid opening D major aria for Goliath (not the usual bass villain but a tenor) uses the trumpets to give heroic atmosphere; the ritornellos in the arias are unusually long, their omission in the reprise hardly surprising; and characterisation by orchestration is not unknown: David sings 'un pastorel son io' in a 3/8 andantino grazioso with *flauti traversi* and *corni da caccia* to support his claim to be rural.

But it is the climax which shows Bertoni's quality. The killing of Goliath occurs in a huge *accompagnato* in which the approach to the fight, the moment of truth and the death of Goliath all have the appropriate musical material. It is necessary to quote the whole scene for its effectiveness to be fully appreciated (example 21).

Ex. 21   Bertoni: *Davidde trionfante di Golia*

Ex. 21 cont.

Ex. 21 cont.

After this large-scale scena, Bertoni feels that the ordinary *lieto fine* chorus is not enough, so he embarks on a series of numbers linked loosely into a group:

Coro: 'S'alzi a Dio voce festiva'
Recit and aria: Saul
Recit and duet: Saul and David
Recit and aria: Saul
Recit: Saul; leading to
Coro: 'S'alzi a Dio' *come sopra*
Coro: *Loda di Gesù*

Bertoni clearly rearranged the libretto to achieve this grand finale for he (or someone) crossed out a first version of 'S'alzi a Dio' and wrote 'si lasa luogo per il Coro'. This last scene, from the fight onwards, shows considerable dramatic and musical flair.

The dating of *Il martirio di S. Cecilia* [67] offers problems since the libretto is unrevealing and the musical material surviving in the Fava library consists only of parts. Caffi's claim[27] that it dates from 1747 is, on the surface, plausible from the libretto's list of 'interlocutori', which seems to have wandered in from an old-fashioned opera seria:

[27] See Zorzi (cited p.77), no. 162.

S. Cecilia
Almachio, tiranno
Valeriano, sposo di S. Cecilia
Fulvio, consigliere

but a closer look at the parts, with arias in a simpler tuneful style, suggests that it may belong to the 1750s, after Galuppi's new manner was known.

Bertoni's next oratorio after *Davidde, L'obbedienza di Gionata* [91], offers no such difficulties. It was given at the Fava in 1756 and, if the presence of a score at Darmstadt is any indication,[28] it gained a more than local fame. The libretto has a particularly operatic look. There is an *argomento* which tells us that 'a number of various episodes' have been added to the biblical story to 'serve the representation' – in other words, to add to the dramatic interest; the author, one Aretuseo Noricio, protests that 'they are in no way sacrilegious' but 'un mero suo abbellimento per adattare il fatto alla Scena'. He then tells us that 'Il presente Dramma comincia dalla sorpresa del Campo Filisteo, e si finge l'azione nelle contrade di Gabaa'. The resemblance to opera is further seen in the Darmstadt score, which is divided into scenes. From this it looks as though the exit convention of opera seria is being obeyed, at least to some extent. Scene VII, for example, has Saul, Gionata and Achinoam. After his aria 'Fra speme, e timore' Saul leaves; Scene VIII is for Gionata and Achinoam, who leaves after his aria 'Sperai felice appieno'; Scene IX is for Gionata alone. His aria 'Del genitor sull'orme' ends the first part. The arias are mainly da capo, some without the ritornello, although there are two examples where there is no reprise. There is a 'Sinfonia lugubre' on the supposed death of Gionata, scored for violins, violas, oboes and horns, which would be equally in place in opera; and the *lieto fine* has all the marks of an operatic dénouement.

It is natural to ask in view of the *argomento* whether in fact there was any intention to stage the work. Certainly in the new church or oratory at the Fava there would have been room to provide some kind of spectacle. Also, there are occasional payments on the sacristy accounts for putting the church in order and for drapes of some kind; but these are just as likely to occur on days when elaborate music other than oratorios was given, so the documentary evidence must be considered inconclusive and indeed against the theory. And as we shall see, when a decade later it becomes quite common for stage directions of various kinds to appear in librettos, they are for the *ospedali* where it would have been virtually impossible to stage them, at least in any meaningful way. So as far as Bertoni's *L'obbedienza di Gionata* is concerned, the safest conclusion may be that composer and librettist were following operatic conventions but not expecting actual operatic performance.

[28] Darmstadt, Hessiche Landes- und Hochschulbibliothek, Mus. ms 104; there is also a score at the Fava.

Opera seria it certainly is, though not in the old style of Jommelli. The arias are not there to show off nimble throats but are in a heavier, more direct manner. Bertoni tends to use the upper registers of the voices rather than fioritura to make his effects (though the tenor singing the part of Saul is taxed at times). He uses the orchestra more extensively and does not spare the voices. Indeed, one can see why a score appears in Germany, for the overture is almost a Mannheim affair, with a fully developed symphonic style and some real crescendos, forte-piano indications and the like. If the climax is not quite as fine as that of *Davidde trionfante di Golia* [79], it is still dramatically effective, the 'Sinfonia lugubre' encasing a good recitative and trio, building up an atmosphere which makes the *lieto fine* seem more than usually out of place.

Bertoni's popularity in Venice is easily understood; and his success at the Mendicanti can be proved by the box office, as it were. The takings of the collecting boxes in the chapel were for many years recorded day by day by the treasurer of the *ospedale*.[29] From these it is clear that the receipts on Good Friday, when his *Miserere* was presumably performed, and on the Feast of St Mary Magdalene, 22 July, were usually higher than on any other day of the year. Not that he did as well as Galuppi. In 1751, Galuppi's last year, the *scagni* for Good Friday totalled 117 lire, those for 22 July, 80 lire. In 1754 Good Friday produced 95 lire, 22 July 91 lire. In 1760 the figures were 76 lire and 87 lire. But in general the position is clear: Bertoni was a popular composer. From these accounts, it is also clear that oratorios did not really pay their way. The members of the 'choir' received half the *scagni* by right. The only expenses apart from this were for copying, which was done by a priest not on the staff of the *ospedale*. Between them, most years, they added up to about 150 lire, compared with the takings of 80 lire. And when the amounts each year were totted up there was usually a deficit on the chapel account. The governors obviously considered this a worthwhile expense; and so it was, considering that the women of the choir attracted foreign pupils and legacies from noble Venetians.

We do not know the financial position of the Fava in such detail, but the oratorio performances continued strongly into the 1760s; and when, on the death of Saratelli in 1762, Bertoni took over as organist and *maestro di cappella*, for several years the position was entirely secure. The repertoire was more catholic than those of the *ospedali*, and there were some revivals of works given or composed either quite a long time earlier or by composers not immediately in the Venetian orbit. Carcani, for example, had succeeded Hasse at the Incurabili, but he had been in Piacenza for about fifteen years when his *Santa Barbara* [99] was repeated at the Fava. Basically a church composer, he writes in a style close to Bertoni's, with relatively heavy and very professional orchestration, many of the arias in the heroic

---

[29] ASV, Ospedali e luoghi pii, Busta 864 and subsequent *buste* of 'cauzioni'.

manner (all are dal segno) and a good conception of the *accompagnato*. Like Bertoni he can think on a broader scale than recitative and aria, writing a grand scena in which a trio is followed straight away by an *accompagnato* leading into a dal segno aria, which returns *subito* into the *accompagnato*; into the last is interposed a *secco* passage. Some of the slower arias are more like the old Neapolitan manner, with triplet figurations and some fioritura. But the 'singers' oratorio has gone and the Neapolitan style is on the way out. A new generation of composers has emerged.

Indeed, by the end of the decade the Venetians had largely reasserted themselves: Bertoni worked at both the Mendicanti and the Fava; Galuppi, after some years composing oratorios for the Incurabili, became their *maestro* in 1768; a young Venetian called Furlanetto took over at the Pietà in the same year; and only at the Ospedaletto do we find foreigners. These were opera composers from Naples, always on the move as usual; and they came to a strange arrangement convenient with both governors and musicians. Traetta was elected in 1766, but two years later he wished to take extended leave to go to Moscow and, rather than give up the post, he found a substitute, Antonio Sacchini; Sacchini in turn by 1773 wished to leave, whereupon Traetta found Pasquale Anfossi, who lasted in effect until the bankruptcy of the *ospedale* in 1777. It has to be said that the governors were not paying any of them very well: 200 ducats at the Ospedaletto (they had to increase it to 400 to keep Traetta), 250 at the Mendicanti, even 400 at the Pietà[30] were not princely salaries, so pluralities of various kinds were to be expected.

In spite of the apparent lack of stability at the Ospedaletto, the arrangement worked out well. All three composers involved turned out to be major composers, and the music for the conservatory which has survived shows them to have given value. Traetta's *Rex Salomon* [378][31] of 1764 is in the opera seria tradition with mainly (though not always) da capo or dal segno arias, sometimes brilliant, sometimes grazioso. Solomon's part, written for Fiorina Vendramin, is taxing and needs a ringing upper register. There are two excellent *accompagnati*, and in general the recitatives show the flair of a true opera composer. The orchestration, though not particularly demanding, is effective. This is an extension of Jommelli's manner, a little plainer in harmony, slightly more sentimental in the slower arias.

Of Sacchini's music for the Ospedaletto, little has survived; in view of his travels in the years when he was substituting for Traetta, we might well wonder how much attention he gave to Venice, though certainly he wrote an oratorio each year. But Anfossi, in spite of gaining fame in the 1770s, did the governors proud. A series of solo

---

[30] Ibid., Busta 694.
[31] Brussels, Bibliothèque Royale de Belgique, ms II 3932.

motets for their singers contains excellent music,[32] and from the several oratorios still extant we can see why he became the celebrity he did. To the history books, he is the composer to whose operas Mozart added additional arias for special singers at Vienna – which in itself reminds us that he was best known for opera buffa (though he also set the usual Metastasio texts). Two of the oratorios, the scores of which we have been able to examine, seem to date from the early 1780s; but there is no reason to postulate a significant change of style from the previous decade, especially since the motets dated from 1775 to 1778 show a distinct resemblance to the oratorios. While *Noe sacrificium* [392] may date from 1773, the extant score[33] is probably later.

Noe sacrificium is unusual in many ways. It has a cast of nine, all women. There is only one da capo aria; and ensembles take up extensive time. The third number, for example, is a kind of chorus-cum-ensemble for the whole cast. The finales for each part are true ensembles, not single chorus-type movements. True, they are not the 'confusion' finales of which da Ponte was a great master, but they use that favourite Mozartian trick of keeping the thematic material going in the orchestra while the voices add their comments with no particularly interesting themes. There is fioritura; but tunes based on simple repeated rhythms, with short-breathed phrases and simple 'natural' modulations, are common. Even the Angel sings thus (example 22). The overture is a *buffo* sinfonia in D major which leads into an *accompagnato* for the Angel. The recitatives are mainly quickly-moving *secco* in style. In fact, opera buffa has arrived in the oratorio.

Ex. 22   Anfossi: *Noe sacrificium*

Violins in unison and thirds with voice

[32] Denis Arnold, 'Pasquale Anfossi's Motets for the Ospedaletto in Venice', *Festschrift Heinrich Hüschen* (Laaber, 1980), pp.17-21.
[33] Venice, Conservatorio di Musica Benedetto Marcello, Fondo Giustinian, B2.7 (15614).

Esther [402] (1781) is little different. True, the cast numbers only six and includes at least two male voices, which may be accounted for by the fact that the available score,[34] which is no more than a partitura for the continuo player, survives in Bologna where there was also a vogue for oratorios. Thus it may not represent the work as heard at the Ospedaletto. There is yet another D major *buffo* overture; then the first 'act' is held together by a chorus 'Viva il re', repeated after short sections of recitative. Esther's music is very florid indeed, as is that of Thamar, who sings a heroic aria with the kind of fioritura shown in example 23. But it is the finales which show Anfossi's experience in

Ex. 23   Anfossi: *Esther*

opera buffa. The one that ends the first part is written as the string of sections common in the 1770s and 80s. It begins with an allegro con brio, using the chorus; there follows an andantino espressivo in F major with three solo sopranos; allegro vivace in A major; andante affetuoso (D major); allegro vivace (A major), and allegro moderato (A major) – the last four sections written for various soloists with choral interpolations. The idiom of these finales as well as most of the arias is close to opera buffa, with short, easily memorable phrases. The mixture of the grand style and this domestic manner reminds us of the same mélange in *Così fan tutte*. There is, as might be expected, none of Mozart's symphonic skill; and it has to be said that whereas the concept of the continuous finale in opera buffa is essentially a way of quickening the dramatic pace, in oratorio it does not add greatly to the feeling of climax. In Anfossi's oratorios the recitatives are very short and the sense of drama is actually less than in many of the earlier works of the opera seria period. It is the idiom of the opera buffa which has been used, not its essential emotional and dramatic structures.

Nevertheless, since the idioms of so many oratorios from the mid-1760s onwards are so close to opera, it is natural to ask whether at least some of them may have been staged. There are, it is true, stage directions in quite a large number of librettos. Traetta's *Rex Salomon* [379], for example (1766 libretto), has 'Salomon in aula, ubi

---

[34] Bologna, Conservatorio di Musica G. B. Martini, CC 198. This must have been used for at least one performance other than the original since there are two different sets of words, one above, one below the stave; and there are many cuts.

thronus est positus'. In Furlanetto's *Joseph* [456], two years later, Thanes and Joseph exit. Bertoni's *Piae virgines choristae* [261] of 1762 has the direction 'pontifices exeuntes moram faciunt' at one point. In his *Parasceve ad sepulturam* [264] there are a number of comings and goings. Galuppi's *Tres pueri Hebraei* [198] of 1774, on the theme of Nebuchadnezzar, has a 'canticum in fornace', while in Furlanetto's *Jerico* [468] of 1775 at the beginning of the second part there is the instruction 'Hic repraesentatur circuitus murorum peractus a sacerdotibus cum arca, & a toto exercitu clangentibus tubis'. There are other more purely musical effects such as distant choruses (Anfossi's *Sedecias* [311]) and military symphonies (Furlanetto's *Triumphus Jephte* [495]).

The most telling evidence against the staging of these oratorios is that all of them were performed at the *ospedali*, not at the Fava. And there was simply no room to stage them, certainly at the Ospedaletto and the Pietà; nor was there at the Mendicanti without a major rearrangement of the musical forces from the normal. (The chapel of the Incurabili is alas no longer there to examine and assess.) At both the Ospedaletto and the new chapel of the Pietà, the choir galleries are surrounded by ironwork which effectively obscures the view of the audience. A recent performance of Anfossi's *Sedecias* in the former proved conclusively that the most that can be seen from the floor of the chapel is the heads of the soloists standing to the front of the gallery. At the Pietà, the two choir galleries are so small that movement as on a stage would be impossible. Indeed, visitors to Venice remarked on the ironwork at these chapels and the invisibility of the performers:[35]

The founders of this charity had, as it appears, too exalted an opinion of the power of music; for, however beautiful the girls may be, they trust only to their melody, being intercepted from the sight of the audience, by a black gauze hung over the rails of the gallery in which they perform: it is transparent enough to shew the figures of women, but not in the least their features or complexion.

This, taken with the lack of any kind of documentary evidence for expenditure on scenery or even drapes (which were known at the Fava), and the fact that at the end of the above-mentioned oratorios of Bertoni the *Miserere* was sung (which surely made them part of a true church service), suggests that these were in no way *spettacoli* like the Viennese *sepolcri* (given with the support of the imperial court). The directions in the librettos acted in the way of the programmes of symphonic poems in the nineteenth century – except that they are rather less essential.

Moreover, the 'operatic' oratorio was not the only type, although it naturally ruled at the Ospedaletto with its visiting *maestri* and at the

---

[35] Samuel Sharp, *Letters from Italy* (2nd edition, London, 1767), p.28.

Mendicanti with Bertoni in control. We do not know Galuppi's later oratorios for the Incurabili, but he had withdrawn from the theatres by the early 1770s and his surviving church music dating from these years is not in an operatic style. And at the Pietà was Furlanetto. Burney and, it seems, Galuppi were not very complimentary about Furlanetto; and looking through the mass of church music he wrote for St Mark's it is not difficult to see why. His *stile antico* is dull in a way that Galuppi's, written earlier, is not. It is still further away from Lotti's flair. The sheer amount of his surviving music is enough to deter the scholar, and to give it a chronology and assess its worth would be a mammoth task.

Nevertheless, Francesco Caffi, writing shortly after Furlanetto's death,[36] gives us the flavour of his reputation in his lifetime. He was appointed *maestro* at the Pietà in 1768 when he was thirty. In the same year he was commissioned (against competition) to write the music for the festival of the canonisation of Girolamo Miani, which took place at S. Maria della Salute; and thereafter he became one of the most sought-after composers for Venetian churches and confraternities, especially the Scuola Grande di S. Rocco. He eventually became organist and finally *maestro di cappella* at St Mark's. Nothing could be further from the career of a composer of opera buffa; and in Caffi's gossipy pamphlet he is praised specifically because 'non profanò la musica sacra colle forme teatrali'.[37]

He had composed several oratorios before his Pietà appointment, and from then until the crisis of 1777 he wrote one almost every year for the *ospedale*. There was then a pause, presumably while the finances of the institution were reorganised, but in the 1780s he resumed the cycle, which continued well into the nineteenth century. If his total oeuvre in the genre is not greater than anyone else's, it must be near it. It would be easy to dismiss such fluency as unlikely to be conducive to good quality; but an examination of the scores surviving mainly in the Pietà collection at the Venice Conservatory shows that he was no negligible composer in his own way.

Which was not the way of Bertoni, still less Anfossi. The most obvious sign of Furlanetto's background and tastes comes early in such a work as *De nativitate virginis* [459], called 'Oratorio secondo' and dated 4 August 1770 in the Conservatory score.[38] There is a written-out organ part – and it is an essential part of the orchestra, being given themes and figures, as are the flutes – and this in spite of a full band, complete with horns and trumpets. Even the organ registration is marked at times, especially in the overture. Not that this shows Furlanetto to be unaware of the resources of the orchestra: the strings have tremolandi, the horns are used for sustained harmonic filling and so on. His modernity also extends to the arias, no

---

[36] Francesco Caffi, *Della vita e del comporre di Buonaventura Furlanetto* (Venice, 1820).
[37] Ibid., p.10.
[38] Venice, Conservatorio di Musica Benedetto Marcello, Fondo Pietà, Busta 68.

longer da capo but through-composed single movements, and developed in short phrases rather than the long-breathed baroque manner (though this does not exclude some brilliant embellished lines).

The same features are to be found in his 'Oratorio quarto' of 1773, *Jaelis victoria* [463],[39] which being intrinsically a more dramatic subject shows Furlanetto's tastes even more sharply. There is a large cast of eight, with the names of the women for whom they are composed added in the score. Again there is a full orchestra, with organ part, and at first it seems as though Furlanetto has some dramatic flair, for the overture breaks off at the end of the second movement and the chorus enters with a 3/8 dance-like movement which essentially replaces the usual finale. The arias are extravagantly virtuosic, with long phrases and elaborate fioritura to show off the skills of the pupils and teachers of the Pietà. But the gross effect is rather a series of movements instead of a drama. The copyist has added the number of bars at the end of various arias: the first has 212, the second 233 and the third 249. These are very long by any standards. There are cadenza points, and the intention to *fare bella figura* is clear. The arias in *David in Siceleg* [469] (1776) or *Reditus exercitus Israelitici* [473] (1777)[40] are much the same; and when the brief perfunctory recitatives are taken into account, the impression of a lack of interest in the drama is conveyed even more strongly. There is some use of the Pietà's divided-choir galleries here and seemingly more chorus than usual (though the available score is only of the first part of the oratorio). It is thus difficult to categorise Furlanetto's oratorios. They are not dramatic yet they are operatic. They resemble the last days of the dying opera seria as seen in Mozart's *Clemenza di Tito*. They are certainly not in a 'church' style, and the music is sometimes interesting, with a touch of real fire.

[39] Ibid., Busta 26.
[40] Ibid., Busta 69. There is no title or composer on the original score, but a note in the typescript catalogue identifies it as *David in Siceleg*; while a card in the score, by Helen Geyer-Kiefl, identifies it as *Reditus exercitus Israel* of 1777.

4
The Last Years of the Most Serene Republic

With hindsight it is easy enough to see that by 1770 Venice was in serious decline. With hindsight and a moral tone it is easy enough to censure the nobility of Venice for not being more industrious or puritanical in life style: 'What of soul was left, I wonder, when the kissing had to stop?'

But Browning, evoking the shade of Galuppi in those days of England's Victorian (and rather smug) security, was not there at the time. The movements which were to destroy the *ancien régime* in France and subsequently in the rest of Europe were not even clouds on the horizon. Did it really seem a time of sunset to the musicians of Venice and their audiences? At the *ospedali*, the minute books of the governors show concern for their income – but when had they not? The crisis, if it seemed real to the officials, can hardly have caused alarm to the *maestri*. At the Pietà, Furlanetto continued to maintain his staff of *maestro di maniera* and *maestro di stromenti*. Anfossi, now very famous, had a *maestro di violino*, an organist and, until 1776 when Gianpallade was pensioned off, a *maestro di maniera*. It was much the same at the Mendicanti with Bertoni still in control; and Galuppi, though now an old man, was still at the Incurabili. There were thus few signs of economies. Indeed, the Mendicanti commissioned a new organ from Callido in 1772 for 300 ducats and the following year decreed that it should have an additional 'registro di trombetti' at a cost of 29 ducats. (A new harpsichord and *spinettone* were also bought that year.) They rewarded Bertoni for good work with a gift of 100 ducats in 1775.

At the Fava in 1769 the fathers regretted that there had been a lack of benefactors to keep the oratorios going without expense falling on the Church, as they had decreed in 1740; but 'given the difficulties [anguiste] of our financial position [it was agreed] to assign 25 ducats to the *prefetto della musica*, leaving him nonetheless at liberty, with the consent of the fathers, to give up to three oratorios, without, however, incurring any other expenses to our congregation'.[1]

---

[1] Fava Archive, Libro de Decreti I, fol.302.

The crash came in 1777. The *ospedali* had gone bankrupt. The reason was simple. As a *supplica* from the governors of the Mendicanti to the Doge puts it, 'for reasons unknown, [income from] the legacies and wills has not been as abundant as in former times, but the poor have not diminished in number'.[2] Although the economies of these institutions have not as yet been thoroughly examined, it is obvious even to the most casual observer of their accounts that they had borrowed freely, from individuals and from the guilds and confraternities, expecting to pay a modest amount of interest on the capital. If such loans were no longer forthcoming they inevitably ran into difficulties. The Mendicanti's *supplica* appealed to the Doge for state intervention; but the state was in a desperate situation itself. Two years earlier, it had tried to raise money by selling admission to the nobility (and hence a seat on the Grand Council). There had been few takers. There could be no salvation from that quarter. The crash at the *ospedali* had far-reaching effects on many people including the fathers at the Fava. At their meeting of 23 April 1777, they discussed ways to reduce expenditure 'in view of the state of our economy, especially in view of the damage caused by the failure [= bankruptcy] of the Ospedale of the Incurabili'.[3] To their credit, they rejected a motion to reduce expenditure on music.

But even with bankruptcies, the needs of the poor and sick went on. The two hundred poor at the Mendicanti could not be turned out onto the streets; the world continued as before. The obvious first step was to reduce expenditure where possible – which meant on music. The Fava may have refused to cut down the number of its musicians, but in fact this would not have made a great deal of difference to its finances. It was different at the *ospedali*. The Pietà was the least affected by the financial climate and, as far as we can find out, the music continued much as before with Furlanetto in charge. Lacking the relevant documents for the Incurabili we are not sure what happened there. At the Ospedaletto, however, the governors decided to cut back all expenditure on musicians, except for an organist who was to teach four girls – clearly in the hope that after three years they could make him redundant.[4] The Mendicanti took a similar line: 'It is resolved that from 1 July until further notice the salary of 350 ducats to the *maestro di musica*, Ferdinando Bertoni, and that of the *maestro di istromenti*, Antonio Martinelli, be suspended.'[5] The girls were henceforth to be taught by the senior members of the choir. But the resolution tells us that the 'benemeriti maestri' wanted to continue to help the *ospedale* and especially its choir 'particularly on the days of the principal solemnities of the *ospedale*...[and to] continue to provide new oratorios, motets and other works'; and above all they

---

[2] Giuseppe Ellero, *Arte e musica all'Ospedaletto* (Venice, 1978), pp.199ff.
[3] Fava Archive, Libro de Decreti I, fol.321.
[4] Ellero, op. cit. (n.2), p.87.
[5] Ibid., p.198.

did not want the introduction of new *maestri*, whether paid or unpaid.

Were the *benemeriti maestri* hoping to take the *scagni* for such days, we may wonder. Or was it simply a matter of goodwill? Bertoni probably had little need of the stipend, considering his post at St Mark's and the receipts from the theatres. Martinelli, on the other hand, was one of the many freelance musicians picking up fees here and there, and cannot have been a wealthy man. Be that as it may, things continued surprisingly as before. In 1778 Bertoni revived his *Abigail* [291] for the Feast of St Mary Magdalene (he called it *Nabal* [293] this time). Furlanetto went on as ever with *Naboth* [474]; and at the Incurabili Ciampi's *Virgines prudentes et fatuae* [202] was given, with the four 'Virgines prudentes' in the first choir and three 'Virgines fatuae' in the second. The following year sees the oratorio flourishing as well as ever, with two pieces by Bertoni at the Mendicanti as well as a dialogue and motets for Mary Magdalene, and Furlanetto as usual at the Pietà. It took a little longer for the Ospedaletto to recover; and, while some of the governors provided funds from their own pockets for music for 1778, it was only in the following decade that their oratorios reappear, first by Anfossi, then from 1782 by their new *maestro* Domenico Cimarosa, a bright young Neapolitan-trained opera composer in the best tradition of the *ospedali*. The casualty, as far as extant librettos and scores indicate, was the Fava, which did occasional revivals of past repertoire but does not seem to have resumed oratorios on its former scale, although a resolution of 12 December 1777 expresses the intention to continue with 'the oratorio in music at Vespertino only on the day of the Epiphany'.[6] The mention of 'vespertino', however, suggests that it was liturgical or paraliturgical music which was performed from now onwards.

So little had changed. Indeed, by 1781 the revival was very strong especially at the Mendicanti, as a poster advertising its musical programme makes plain:[7]

NOTICE
IN THE CHURCH OF THE MENDICANTI
LENT OF THE YEAR 1781

March

2	Friday	Sacred Dialogue: Canticorum Sponsa [304], and Miserere by Signor Maestro Ferdinando Bertoni
4	Sunday	Oratorio: Bethulia Liberata [303] by Signor Maestro Felice Alessandri
9	Friday	Stabat Mater: of Pergolesi, and Pange Lingua for a solo voice

---

[6] Fava Archive, Libro de Decreti I, fol.324.
[7] Venice, Biblioteca Casa di Goldoni, 59F 12/1.

11	Sunday	Oratorio: de Morte Sisarae [*306*] by Signor Gio. Giacomo Avanzini
16	Friday	Sacred Dialogue: Jonathas [*308*], and Miserere by Signor Maestro Bertoni
18	Sunday	Oratorio: Mors Athaliae [*305*] by Signor Maestro Bertoni
19	Monday	Oratorio: Poenitentia David [*307*] by Signor Maestro Bertoni
23	Friday	Stabat Mater, and Pange Lingua
25	Sunday	Oratorio: Bethulia Liberata by Signor Maestro Alessandri
30	Friday	Sacred Dialogue: Canticorum Sponsa and Miserere by Signor Maestro Bertoni
April		
1	Sunday	Vacation
6	Friday	Stabat Mater, and Pange Lingua
8	Sunday	New Oratorio: Baltassar [*302*]: by Signor Maestro Bertoni, and Miserere
9	Monday	
10	Tuesday	
11	Wednesday	Office and Miserere
12	Thursday	
13	Friday	

The repertoire, it will be noted, is not particularly new: one novelty by Bertoni, most of his works being revivals; Avanzini (organ teacher at the Ospedaletto from 1761 to 1770, or possibly his son who acted as his deputy in 1768) can hardly have been very advanced by Venetian tastes; while Felice Alessandri (a successful composer of opera buffa) seems to have written his Metastasian oratorio for a private performance in Padua. Little of this music can have required copying anew (an expensive business on this scale) though the strain on the girls' rehearsal time must have been considerable. In any case, this veritable festival is evidence of the liveliness of the Mendicanti even in its state of having no paid music staff.

We have no other such posters; but the evidence is that throughout the decade oratorio performances continued to be popular. Goethe went to the Mendicanti in October 1786:[8]

Here is the Conservatorio, which at the present time enjoys the highest reputation. The women were singing an oratorio behind the choir screen: the church was filled with listeners, the music beautiful and the voices superb. An alto sang the part of King Saul, the protagonist in the work. I have never heard such a voice. Some passages in the music were of infinite beauty and the text was perfectly singable – a kind of Italian Latin which made one smile at times but which gave the music wide scope.

We have no direct record of this performance, but it seems likely that it was a revival of *Triumphus David de Goliat gigante* [*315*] by Giuseppe

[8] Johann Wolfgang von Goethe, *Italian Journey (1786-88)*, trans. W. H. Auden and Elisabeth Mayer (London, 1962), p.67.

Mauroceno, first performed at the Mendicanti in 1783, in which case Goethe probably heard two of the stars of the conservatory, Theresia Almerigo as Saul and Antonia Lucovich as Michal and Joab. They were both old singers (Almerigo had over twenty years' experience of singing oratorio). Goethe's comment on the Latin (he may well have had a libretto) is very apt. The Latin of the oratorio texts is indeed a sort of Metastasian version of the ancient language, and thus very suitable for setting to music.

Little need be said of the musical style of this last phase of the Venetian oratorio. The scores by Furlanetto do not show any significant change, although there are differences between works. *De solemni Balthassar* [492] of 1787, for example,[9] uses double choir and orchestra, the six soloists divided into two groups, obviously to exploit the Pietà's separated galleries. The arias are similar to those in his earlier works, partly virtuosic, partly in a more 'short phrases' style. The first-part finale is sectional in the way of opera buffa without in any way belonging to a *buffo* style. Furlanetto's scoring is now bolder and more competent, this showing especially in *Absalonis rebellio* [485] of 1785[10] with its 'victory' finale putting trumpets and drums to good use and a 'traversa obligo Sra Anna Maria Ochizari' of some elaboration. By 1792 he was capable of a regular northern-style *sinfonia* for the overture to *Gedeon* [497],[11] complete with a slow introduction to the first movement and a finale weightier than the usual Italian 3/8 dance.

While Furlanetto continued to write his oratorios specially for the women of the Pietà, it is noticeable that the repertoire elsewhere was mainly by composers outside the orbit of the *ospedali*. Most of these are indeed nonentities, but one of the most popular figures, Giuseppe Gazzaniga, who had been organ teacher at the Ospedaletto for about two years from 1770, was a more considerable figure. To judge from his oratorio *S. Mauro*,[12] which was admittedly probably not composed for Venice, he favoured an opera buffa style, the arias rather direct and simple in melody, one even being called 'cavatina'. The penultimate number is marked 'rondo' for the principal soloist, Mauro, and the finale is a quartet rather than a 'coro' in the old way. It is a piece which would have gone down well at the Fava, lacking the necessity for great virtuosity but dramatically effective and with pleasant music.

This score does not suggest much change in taste from the 1770s in Venice and neither do Furlanetto's later oratorios; but there are two settings of Metastasio's *Passion* that hint that a more advanced music was creeping into Venice. Certainly we cannot prove that either was performed there, but circumstantial evidence suggests that both may

---

[9] Venice, Conservatorio di Musica Benedetto Marcello, Fondo Pietà, Busta 26.
[10] Ibid.
[11] Ibid.
[12] Bologna, Conservatorio di Musica G. B. Martini, ms 77104.

well have been. Andrea Lucchesi's setting survives along with much of his music in the library of the d'Este family, dukes of Modena;[13] but his connections in early life with the Incurabili and his presence in Venice in 1783-4 suggest a possible performance then, especially since the surviving orchestral material is much in line with Venetian circumstances rather than the somewhat grander conditions at a ducal court. The setting by Paisiello, a famous work indeed, exists today in Venice in two copies, the one in the Marciana[14] admittedly a twentieth-century acquisition (though probably from a local Venetian source), the other, in the library of the Istituzioni di Ricovero e di Educazione, surely deriving from either an *ospedale* or a Venetian church. Both works show a move away from the old line of Metastasian passion music. Both show a much crisper idea of melody, Lucchesi's arias having a little fioritura, Paisiello's still less. Both take Metastasio's provision of opportunities for *recitativo accompagnato* to heart, Paisiello running them into the succeeding aria to form a continuous complex. Paisiello's use of the chorus is especially skilled, the final chorus being called 'preghiera' and marked 'sotto voce' and using chromaticisms to good effect. Indeed the whole style of his *Passion* might be called 'post-Gluck', since Paisiello has diminished the role of secco recitative very considerably. This seems the natural successor to the old opera seria-type oratorios and, in the mormal way, this frenchified Italian manner might have given fresh life to the oratorio.

If such works were being performed in the last years of the Venetian Republic the fact should warn us against easy equations between the decadence of society and its artistic manifestations. Indeed the quality and seriousness of the oratorios given in Venice is so much at odds with the reputation of a society given over to the pleasures of the carnival, the *ridotto* and the like that we should clearly give up simple moralising; and the nature of eighteenth-century Venetian church music in general is such that we should be even more cautious about accepting the view of the Serenissima as a worldly, godless society.

Napoleon defeated Venice not because it was decadent but because it was militarily weak. Its grand musical tradition perished not because it reflected the vigourless society around it but because the institutions which gave it substance were largely destroyed. That they were not completely destroyed is proved by the renewed theatrical activity around the recently built Teatro La Fenice, which was to see in the work of Rossini, though it is significant that Venetian opera was now eclipsed by that of the even more decadent society of Naples, simply because the Teatro S. Carlo was supported amply by the state.

---

[13] Modena, Biblioteca Estense, F.648 (1–25). For a survey of the composer's life and works, including an analysis of the Passion on pp.182-97, see Claudia Valer-Knechtges, *Die Kirchenmusik Andrea Luchesis* (Cologne, 1983).

[14] Venice, Biblioteca Nazionale Marciana, It. IV. 701-2 [= 10380-1].

As far as oratorio was concerned, Furlanetto continued to the end of his life at the Pietà, producing a new work or revising old ones each year. The other *ospedali*, now joined together for administrative reasons, were no longer active as musical institutions. The Filippini managed to survive at the Fava until the monastic orders were suppressed in 1810.[15] When they returned to the church in 1821, they revived their musical traditions with some success, but oratorio was not among their activities. So ended a distinguished chapter in Italian musical history. If much of the music given by the *ospedali* has perished, much remains in a quiet room of the Padri Redentori behind the Fava church. It must be hoped that musicians will increasingly seek out its treasures and allow us to hear some of the glories of eighteenth-century Venice.

[15] Paolo Pancino, *Venezia: S. Maria della Consolazione* (Milan, 1969), p.5.

Appendix

Oratorios performed in Venice 1662-1809

This appendix attempts to list all the oratorios that can be documented as having been performed in Venice during the above years.

Abbreviations:

L	location(s) of printed libretto (using RISM sigla)
S	location(s) of manuscript score (using RISM sigla; * denotes an autograph)
N	notes, references or documentation, using the following abbreviations:

Allacci	Lione Allacci, *Drammaturgia divisa in sette indici*, rev. G. B. Pasquali (Venice, 1755)
Busta	Venice, Archivio di Stato, Filippini, relevant *busta* number
Caffi	Francesco Caffi, 'Materiali e carteggi per la storia della musica teatrale', in Venice, Biblioteca Nazionale Marciana, ms It. cl. IV. 747 (=10462-5)
Cini	Library of the Fondazione Cini, Isola di S. Giorgio, Venice
Girardi	*Il tranquillo seren del secol d'oro* (Venice and Milan, 1984), chapter by Maria Girardi
IRE	Archive of the Istituzioni di Ricovero e di Educazione, Venice
NG	*The New Grove Dictionary of Music and Musicians*, ed. Stanley Sadie (London, 1980)
PV	*Pallade veneta*: see *Pallade veneta: Writings on Music in Venetian Society*, ed. Eleanor Selfridge-Field (Venice, 1985)
Schmidl	Carlo Schmidl, *Dizionario universale dei musicisti* (Milan, 1926, supplement 1938)
Zorzi	Maria Antonietta Zorzi, 'Saggio di bibliografia sugli oratorii sacri eseguiti a Venezia', in *Accademie e biblioteche d'Italia*, iv (1930-1), pp.226-46, 394-403, 529-43; v (1931-2), pp.79-96, 493-508; vi (1932-3), pp.256-69; vii (1933-4), pp.316-41

i: Fava (S. Maria della Consolazione detta Della Fava)
(singers' names never given)

No.	Date	Title (Librettist if known)	Composer
1	1671	Sedecia	G. Legrenzi
	L I-Mb *S* I-Rvat *N* Busta 63		
2	1671	Oratorio della passione	G. Legrenzi?
	N Busta 63		
3	1672	L'huomo moribondo	?
	N Busta 68		

No.	Date	Title (Librettist if known)	Composer
4	1672	Creation del mondo	G. Legrenzi
	N Busta 68		
5	1672	Giudizio (I. Bentivogli)	G. Legrenzi
	L I-Vnm; A-SPL *N* Busta 68; dated 1668 in A-SPL		
6	1672	Moisè	G. Legrenzi
	N Busta 68		
7	1672	Sedecia	G. Legrenzi
	N Busta 68; see no. 1		
8	1672	Sisara	G. Legrenzi
	L I-Mb *N* Busta 68		
9	1673	L'huomo moribondo	?
	N Busta 68; see no. 3		
10	1673	Moisè	G. Legrenzi
	N Busta 68; see no. 6		
11	1673	La morte del cor penitente	G. Legrenzi
	L A-Wn *S* A-Wn		
12	1673	Peccator pentito	?
	N Busta 68		
13	1673	S. Giovanni Battista	G. Legrenzi?
	N Busta 68		
14	1673	Salamone	?
	N Busta 68		
15	1673	La vendita del cuor humano *or* Il cuore humano all'incanto	G. Legrenzi/ P. A. Ziani
	S I-MOe; Rvat *N* Busta 68 *S* I-Nf		
16	1674	Adamo et Eva	G. Legrenzi?
	N Busta 64		
17	1674	La vendita del cuor humano	G. Legrenzi/ P. A. Ziani
	N Busta 64; see no. 15		
18	1674	S. Giovanni Battista	G. Legrenzi?
	N Busta 64; see no. 13		
19	1674	Sedecia	G. Legrenzi
	N Busta 64; see no. 1		
20	1675	Gli sponsali d'Ester	G. Legrenzi
	L I-Vnm *N* Busta 68; libretto for perf. in 1676 in Bologna?		
21	1675	Lo sposalito di Rebecca	?
	L I-Vnm		
22	1677	Sisara	G. Legrenzi
	N Girardi, p.167		
23	1683	Abramo vincitore	G. A. Perti
	N NG		
24	1689?	La morte del giusto (B. Sandrinelli)	G. A. Perti
	L I-Bc; Mb *S* I-Bsp		
25	1696	Il cuor nello scrigno (F. Arisi)	B. Vinacesi
	N NG		
26	1696	Il cuore umano	G. Legrenzi/ P. A. Ziani
	L I-BGc		

No.	Date	Title (Librettist if known)	Composer
27	1696 N Busta 68	L'huomo moribondo	?
28	1696 L I-Mb	Oloferne	?
29	1697 L I-Vsmc N 'tragedia spirituale'	Il combattimento degli angioli (G. F. Roberti)	C.F. Pollarolo
30	1697 L I-Vnm	Il figliuol prodigo (R. Ciallis)	A. Biffi
31	1697 S I-Rvat N see no. 1	Sedecia	G. Legrenzi
32	1697 L I-Vnm	Il trionfo della continenza (B. Sandrinelli)	A. Caldara
33	1698 L I-Mb; Rn	I disegni della divina sapienza (C. F. Belli Badia)	B. Sabbadini
34	1698 L I-Vnm S A-Wn	Il giudizio di Salomone (R. Cial- lis)	M. A. Ziani
35	1698 L I-Mb S D-MÜs	Il ricco epulone (B. Sandrinelli)	A. Caldara
36	1698 L I-Mb	Santa Pelagia	M. A. Ziani
37	1699 L I-BGc	La decollazione di S. Giovanni Battista	?
38	1700? L I-Pu	L'impenitente ravveduto	?
39	1701? L I-Mb; Rsc	Sansone accecato de' Filistei (B. Sandrinelli)	F. A. Urio
40	1704 L I-Vnm N see no. 30	Il figliuol prodigo (R. Ciallis)	A. Biffi
41	1705 L I-Vnm N see no. 11	La morte del cor penitente	G. Legrenzi
42	1740 L I-Vnm; Rsc; Ma S I-Vsmc	La circoncisione del santo bambino	P. V. Chiocchetti
43	1740 L I-Vcg; Pu; Mb S I-Vsmc as L'impenitente peccatore	L'impenitente ravveduto	?
44	1740 N Zorzi 239	S. Maurizio e compagni martiri	B. Galuppi
45	1741 L I-Vnm S I-Vsmc; GB-Lbm	S. Francesco di Sales	F. Feo
46	1741 N perf. 1 Jan (Allacci)	Isaaco, figura del redentore (P. Metastasio)	A. Coletti
47	1741 L I-Vnm; Mb	La morte di Abele	D. Valentini

No.	Date	Title (Librettist if known)	Composer

48 1741   La morte di Abele (P. Metastasio)   L. Leo
L I-Vsmc; Vcg; Cini; Vnm; Rsc; PAc   *S* I-Vsmc; Bc; Nc; A-Wn; B-Bc; D-Bds; Dlb; Mbs

49 1742   Il Giuseppe riconosciuto   P. Scalabrini
                (P. Metastasio)
L I-Vcg; Vmc; Mb   *S* I-Vsmc

50 1742   Isacco figura del redentore   N. Jommelli
                (P. Metastasio)
L I-Vcg; Vsmc (1764)   *S* many scores including I-Vsmc; Bc; Fc; Vnm; GB-Lbm; Lcm; T

51 1742   S. Atanasio patriarca di   M. Bisso
                Alessandria
L I-Vsmc (1742); Ma; Mb; PAc; Rsc; Vcg; Cini   *S* I-Vsmc (1741)

52 1743   La passione di Gesù Cristo   N. Conti
                (P. Metastasio)
L I-Mb; Rsc   *S* I-Vsmc

53 1743   La passione di Gesù Cristo   D. Valentini
                (P. Metastasio)
L I-Vcg; Rsc

54 1743   Jaele   N. Sabbatino
L I-Vcg; Rsc; Vsmc; Cini   *S* I-Vsmc

55 1743   Il martirio di S. Cecilia   G. Petrodusio
L I-Vnm; Vsmc   *S* I-Vsmc (parts)

56 1744   S. Elena al Calvario (P. Meta- L. Leo
                stasio)
L I-Vcg; Vsmc; Ma; Cini   *S* many scores incl. I-Vsmc; Nc; A-Wn; B-Bc; D-Bds; GB-Cfm

57 1744   Per la festività del SS.mo natale P. Chiarini
                (P. Metastasio)
L I-Vsmc; Vcg; Mb; Rsc; Vnm; Cini

58 1745   Assalone riconciliato col padre   M. Bisso
L I-Vcg; Mb; Rsc; Ma   *S* I-Vsmc

59 1745   Il martirio di S. Cecilia   G. Petrodusio
N see no. 55

60 1745   I pellegrini al sepolcro   J. A. Hasse
L I-Vcg; Vsmc; Vnm; Vmc; Cini   *S* many scores incl. I-Vsmc; Bc; *Mc; Vnm; GB-Er; Lbm; Lcm; T; US-Bp; NH; PRu; Wc   *N* published by J. A. Hiller (Leipzig, 1784)

61 1746   La circoncisione del santo   P. V. Chiocchetti
                bambino Gesù
N see no. 42; Zorzi

62 1746   La fuga dal secolo   G. B. Costanzi
L I-Vsmc; Vcg; Cini; Ma; Mb; Vnm

63 1746   Ortus in praedio Gethsemani   F. Bertoni
N NG (no place of perf. given)

64 1746   Santa Barbara   G. Carcani
L I-Vsmc; Vcg; Vnm; Cini   *S* I-Vsmc

65 1746   S. Francesco di Sales   F. Feo
L I-Vsmc; Vcg   *N* see no. 45

66 1747   Jaele   N. Sabbatino
N see no. 54; Zorzi

No.	Date	Title (Librettist if known)	Composer

67 1747? Il martirio di S. Cecilia F. Bertoni
L I-Vcg; Vsmc *S* I-Vsmc (parts) *N* see pp.61-2 for discussion of dating

68 1747 Il ritorno del figliuol prodigo F. Bertoni
L I-Mb; Cini *S* I-Bc; Vsmc

69 1748 Adamo caduto (P. Metastasio) B. Galuppi
L I-Vsmc; Vnm; Mb; Rsc *S* I-Vsmc; Vnm; Tn ('Adamo ed Eva')

70 1748 Gesù nato (G. Terribilini) A. Bencini
L I-Rsc (1760) *S* I-Vsmc

71 1749 Gesù adorato da' re magi M. Bisso
L I-Vsmc; Mb *S* I-Vsmc

72 1749 L'innocenza rispettata A. G. Pampani
L I-Vcg *S* I-Vsmc

73 1749 La passione di Gesù Cristo N. Conti
N see no. 52; Zorzi

74 1749 La passione di Gesù Cristo N. Jommelli
(P. Metastasio)
S I-Vnm *N* composed 1749 for Rome/Naples; date of Fava perf. unknown

75 1750 La circoncisione del santo bam- P. V. Chiocchetti
bino
N see no. 42; Zorzi

76 1750 Il Giuseppe riconosciuto P. Scalabrini
N Caffi; see no. 49

77 1750? Il martirio di Santa Cecilia F. Turini
L I-Vcg; Vsmc; Vnm; Cini; C-Tu

78 1750? Pastorale per la natività di Gesù G. Carcani
Cristo
L I-Vsmc (n.d.)

79 1751? Davidde trionfante di Golia F. Bertoni
L I-Mb; Rsc; Cini; Vnm; B-Br *S* I-Vsmc; Mc

80 1751? Salomone re d'Israele A. Bergamo
L I-Vcg; Vnm; Rsc; Cini; C-Tu *S* I-Vsmc

81 1752 S. Maurizio e compagni martiri A. G. Pampani
L I-Vnm; Vsmc; Cini; Mb *S* I-Vsmc

82 1753? Gioas re di Giuda (P. Metastasio) F. Corbisiero
L I-Vsmc; Vmc *S* I-Vsmc

83 1753 S. Antonio da Padova F. Durante
L I-Vsmc; Rsc; Cini; Mb *S* I-Vsmc; Vnm

84 1753 La sposa de' sacri cantici B. Furlanetto
L I-Vmc; Cini; Chioggia, Biblioteca comunale *S* I-Bc; Chioggia, Oratory of St Philip Neri

85 1754 S. Antonio da Padova F. Durante
N see no. 83; NG

86 1754 Assalone riconciliato col padre M. Bisso
L I-Vcg *N* see no. 58

87 1754 S. Barbara G. Carcani
N see no. 64; Zorzi

88 1754 Il ritorno del figliuol prodigo F. Bertoni
L I-Fm; Rsc; Cini *N* see no. 68

No.	Date	Title (Librettist if known)	Composer
89	1755?	La passione di Gesù Cristo (P. Metastasio)	N. Jommelli

L Chioggia, Biblioteca comunale *S* many scores incl. I-Bc; Mc; Nc; Vnm; Vsmc; GB-Lbm; Lgc; US-BE *N* libretto for perf. in Rome

| 90 | 1755 | I pellegrini al sepolcro | J. A. Hasse |

L I-Vsmc *N* see no. 60

| 91 | 1756 | L'obbedienza di Gionata (A. Noricio) | F. Bertoni |

L I-Vcg; Vsmc; Cini; Mb; PAc; Rsc; C-Tu *S* I-Vsmc; Vnm; D-DS

| 92 | 1756 | Il sagrificio di Jefte | B. Galuppi |

L I-Vnm; Vsmc; Rsc; C-Tu *S* I-Vsmc

| 93 | 1756 | S. Elena al Calvario | L. Leo |

L I-Vcg *N* see no. 56

| 94 | 1756 | S. Francesco di Sales | F. Feo |

L I-Vnm *N* see no. 45

| 95 | 1757? | Il Giuseppe riconosciuto (P. Metastasio) | J. A. Hasse |

L I-Vsmc; Vcg; Cini; Vnm; Mb; C-Tu *S* I-Vsmc; *Mc; Vnm; GB-Er; D-Dlb *N* libretto n.d.; 1757? (NG)

| 96 | 1758 | Betulia liberata (P. Metastasio) | N. Jommelli |

L I-Vsmc; Fm; Mb; Rsc; Chioggia, Biblioteca comunale *S* many scores incl. I-Mc; Nc; Vsmc; GB-Lbm; D-MÜs

| 97 | 1758 | La circoncisione del santo bambino | P. V. Chiocchetti |

L I-Vsmc; Vcg *N* see no. 42

| 98 | 1760 | Gesù nato | A. Bencini |

L I-Rsc *N* see no. 70

| 99 | 1760 | Santa Barbara | G. Carcani |

L I-Vcg *N* see no. 64

| 100 | 1762? | La deposizione dalla croce (G. Pasquini) | F. Turini |

L I-Vcg; Vsmc; Cini; Vnm; Rsc; Mb *S* I-Vsmc *N* libretto dated 1762 in ms, I-Vmc

| 101 | 1763 | Jaele componimento sacro | N. Sabbatino |

L I-Vmc *N* see no. 54

| 102 | 1763 | S. Antonio da Padova | F. Durante |

L I-Vsmc *N* see no. 83

| 103 | 1764 | Isacco | N. Jommelli |

L I-Vsmc *N* see no. 50

| 104 | 1765 | L'innocenza rispettata | A. G. Pampani |

L I-Vsmc *N* see no. 72

| 105 | 1767 | La sposa de' sacri cantici | B. Furlanetto |

L I-Vmc; Cini; Chioggia, Oratory of St Philip Neri *S* I-Bc; Chioggia, Oratory of St Philip Neri

| 106 | 1768 | Il martirio di S. Cecilia | G. Petrodusio |

S I-Vsmc *N* in tenor part: 'sung 2 Feb 1767': see no. 55

| 107 | 1773 | La sposa de' sacri cantici | B. Furlanetto |

L I-Vmc *N* see no. 84

| 108 | 1785 | Betulia liberata | N. Jommelli |

L I-Vsmc *N* see no. 96; in libretto: 'shortened to its present form owing to the circumstances of the singers'; only 4 characters instead of 6 or 8

No.	Date	Title (Librettist if known)	Composer
109	1787 *L* I-Vsmc *N* see no. 68	Il ritorno del figliuol prodigo	F. Bertoni
110	1787 *N* NG	Il Giuseppe riconosciuto (P. Metastasio)	F. Bertoni
111	1789 *N* NG	Assalone	A. Baldan
112	n. d. *L* I-Vsmc; Vnm *N* 'cantate morali'	Componimenti sacri per musica	?

(There are many more repeat performances listed in Caffi and Zorzi for which librettos have not been traced.)

ii: Incurabili (Ospedale degli Incurabili)

113	1677 *N* Caffi	S. Francesco Saverio (C. Badoer?)	C. Pallavicino
114	1680 *L* I-Mb	Le allegrezze di Maria vergine	?
115	1680 *L* I-Mb	La Maddalena penitente	?
116	1686 *N* Allacci	Maria Maddalena	C. Pallavicino
117	1687 *L* I-Bam; Mb; Rsc *N* perf. 12 Jan (PV)	Il trionfo dell'innocenza (F. M. Piccioli)	C. Pallavicino
118	c. 1687? *N* n. d. (Allacci)	Fuga trionfante nella nascita, vita e morte di Santa Teresa (F. M. Piccioli)	?
119	1688 *L* I-Fn; Vcg	Clotilde (F. M. Piccioli)	?
120	1688 *N* perf. Feb (PV)	La Spagna convertita	C. Pallavicino
121	1688 *L* I-Rsc (ms) *N* perf. Feb (PV)	Iberia convertita	C. Pallavicino
122	1688 *N* PV; repeat of no. 116?	Maria Maddalena	C. Pallavicino
123	1694 *L* I-Vcg	L'indice della penitenza	?
124	1701? *N* n. d. (Caffi)	Gioas re di Giuda (Z. Vallaresso)	A. Lotti
125	1701? *N* n. d. (Caffi)	Judith	A. Lotti
126	1701 *L* I-Rsc	La Maddalena penitente	?
127	1702 *N* perf. April (PV)	Anima afflitta et consolata	F. Gasparini

No.	Date	Title (Librettist if known)	Composer
128	1702	Conversio gloriosa	?
	L I-Vcg; Rsc		
129	1702	S. Romualdo	A. Lotti
	N perf. 7 Oct (PV)		
130	1702	Sant'Orsola	C. F. Pollarolo
	N PV		
131	1703	Tertius crucis triumphus	C. F. Pollarolo
	L I-BGc; Vnm; Rsc		
132	1704	Animae errantio conversio	?
	N Caffi		
133	1704	Christus in Golgotha	?
	N Caffi		
134	1704	Conversio gloriosa in vita Divinae Ursulae	C. F. Pollarolo
	N perf. 1 March (PV)		
135	1704	Divini amoris victoria	?
	L I-Vmc; Ma; Rsc; Vnm		
136	1704	Hierosolimae urbis excidium	?
	N Caffi		
137	1704?	Super psalmum Deus in nomine tuo	?
	L I-Vnm; Vmc; both ms N singers' names in I-Vmc		
138	1704	La vittoria dell'amor divino	C. F. Pollarolo
	N PV		
139	1706	Samson vindicatus	C. F. Pollarolo
	L I-Vcg; Rsc S GB-Mp ('Sansone')		
140	1707	Joseph in Aegypto	C. F. Pollarolo
	L I-Mb; Vcg; Rsc N singers' names in ms, I-Vcg		
141	1712	Triumphus fidei	A. Lotti
	L I-Vcg; Vnm; Rsc		
142	1714	Recognitio fratrum	A. Pollarolo
	L I-Vcg; Rsc		
143	1716	Rex regum	C. F. Pollarolo
	L I-Vcg; Vmc; Rsc		
144	1718	Davidis de Goliath triumphus	C. F. Pollarolo
	L I-Rsc; Vcg		
145	1726-33	Introductio ad psalmum	N. Porpora
	L I-Vmc (ms) N singers' names		
146	1726-33	Introductio ad psalmum Miserere	N. Porpora
	L I-Vmc N characters different from no. 145		
147	1726-33	Oratorio	?
	L I-Vnm (ms) N singers' names		
148	1730-3	Christus Dominus in serpente or Serpentes in deserto	J. A. Hasse
	L I-Vmc S A-Wn; D-B; Dlb; Mbs; F-Pc; I-Vc; US-Wc N singers' names		
149	1730-3	S. Petrus et S. Maria Magdalena	J. A. Hasse
	L I-Vnm; Vmc; Rsc S A-Wn; CH-Zz; D-B; Dlb; LEm; GB-Er; T N ends with Miserere		
150	1733	Sanctus Petrus Urseolus	N. Porpora
	L I-Vcg; Vnm (ms) N singers' names in I-Vnm		

No.	Date	Title (Librettist if known)	Composer

(From here onwards, all librettos print singers' names.)

151	1733?	solo motets	?

L I-Vnm (ms) *N* singers' names in I-Vnm

152	1745	Joas (P. Metastasio)	N. Jommelli

L I-Vcg; Vnm; Rsc; Bl *S* I-Ac (different version)

153	1746?	Christo defuncto exequie	?

L I-Vnm + ms

154	1746?	Iuda proditor (J. de Bellis)	N. Jommelli

L I-Vmc (ms)

155	1746	Modulamina sacra	N. Jommelli

L I-Vcg

156	1747	Bethulia liberata (P. Metastasio)	V. Ciampi

L I-Vnm; Rsc *N* Latin trans.

157	1748	Christus a morte quaesitus	V. Ciampi

L I-Vnm (ms)

158	1749	Sanctus Petrus Urseolus	N. Porpora

L I-Rsc *N* see no. 150

159	1753	Carmina sacra	G. Cocchi

L I-Rsc

160	1753	Joas	N. Jommelli

L I-Vnm; Pci; Rn *N* see no. 152

161	1754	Petri contritio	G. Cocchi

L I-Vcg; Vnm; Cini; Rsc

162	1754	Sacer dialogus	G. Cocchi

L I-Vnm *N* solo motets

163	1755	Abel occisus	G. Cocchi

L I-Vnm; Rsc *N* ends with Miserere

164	1755	Joas	N. Jommelli

L I-Vnm *N* see no. 152

165	1755	Divinae hypostasis encomium	G. Cocchi

L I-Rsc; Vnm

166	1756	Jerusalem ad Christum Dominum	G. Cocchi

L I-Vcg; Rsc; VIb

167	1756	Sermo apostolicus	G. Cocchi

L I-Vnm; Rsc; Cini

168	1757	Mons divinae claritatis	G. Cocchi

L I-Vcg; Vnm; Cini; Rsc

169	1757	Noe	G. Cocchi

L I-Vcg; Vnm; Rsc *N* 'drama sacrum'; ends with Miserere

170	1758	S. Petrus et S. Maria Magdalena	J. A. Hasse

L I-Vmc *N* see no. 149

171	1759	Israel ab Aegyptiis liberatus	N. Porpora

L I-Vcg; Vnm; Rsc *S* GB-Lbm 2 arias

172	1760	Carmina sacra	V. Ciampi

L I-Vcg *N* solo motets

173	1760	Virgines prudentes et fatuae	V. Ciampi

L I-Vcg; Vnm; Rsc

174	1761	Sacra modulamina	V. Ciampi

L I-Vnm; PAc; MAC

No.	Date	Title (Librettist if known)	Composer
175	1761	Vexillum fidei cecinerunt	V. Ciampi
		L I-Vnm; Vcg; Pu; Rsc *N* ends with Miserere	
176	1762	Vexillum fidei cecinerunt	V. Ciampi
		N see no. 175	
177	1763	Maria Magdalena introductio ad psalmum (P. Chiari?)	B. Galuppi
		L I-Vcg; Vnm; Rsc	
178	1763	Sacer dialogus arcangelum inter Michaelem	?
		L I-Vcg; Vnm *N* solo motets	
179	1764?	Modulamina sacra	G. F. Brusa
		L I-Vnm *N* dated by singers' names	
180	1764	Sacrificium Abraham introductio ad psalmum Miserere (P. Chiari?)	B. Galuppi
		L I-Vcg	
181	1764	Trasfiguratio dominica (P. Chiari?)	B. Galuppi
		L I-Vnm	
182	1765	Triumphus divini amoris (P. Chiari?)	B. Galuppi
		L I-Vcg; Vmc; Rsc	
183	1765	Vexillum fidei cecinerunt	V. Ciampi
		L I-Vnm *N* see no. 175	
184	1766	Redemptionis veritas	G. F. Brusa
		L I-Vcg; Vnm; Rsc; Pu	
185	1767	Aeternum humanae reparationis	G. F. Brusa
		L I-Vcg; Vnm; Rsc *N* 'drama sacrum'	
186	1767	Coelum apertum in transfiguratione Domini	G. F. Brusa
		L I-Vcg; Vnm; Rsc; Ma *N* 'modi sacri'	
187	1767-76?	Sacer trialogus	A. Lucchesi
		L I-Vmc (ms) *N* dated by singers' names	
188	1768	Abrahae revocati in gloria Christi	G. F. Brusa
		N Schmidl	
189	1768	Manes justorum a sinu Abrahae	G. F. Brusa
		L I-Vcg; Vc; Rsc; PAc	
190	1769	Tres Mariae ad sepulchrum (P. Chiari?)	B. Galuppi
		L I-Vnm; Pu; Rsc	
191	1770	Canticorum sponsi (P. Chiari?)	B. Galuppi
		L I-Vcg; Vmc	
192	1770-1?	Nuptiae Rachelis (P. Chiari?)	B. Galuppi
		L I-Vcg; Vmc	
193	1770	Parabola coenae (P. Chiari?)	B. Galuppi
		L I-Vcg; Vnm	
194	1771	Adam (P. Chiari after Klopstock)	B. Galuppi
		L I-Vcg	
195	1771	Dialogus sacer (P. Chiari?)	B. Galuppi
		L I-Vmc	
196	1772	Debbora prophetissa (P. Chiari?)	B. Galuppi
		L I-Vmc	

No.	Date	Title (Librettist if known)	Composer

197 1773   Daniel in lacu leonum (P. Chiari?) B. Galuppi
L I-Vcg; Pu; Rsc

198 1774   Tres pueri Hebraei (P. Chiari?)   B. Galuppi
L I-Vcg; Vnm

199 1775   Exitus Israelis de Aegypto   B. Galuppi
                (P. Chiari?)
L I-Vmc; Vcg *S* I-Gi(l) fragment

200 1776   Moyses (P. Chiari)   B. Galuppi
L I-Vcg; Pu; Rsc

201 1776   Mundi salus (P. Chiari?)   B. Galuppi
L I-Vcg; Pu

202 1778   Virgines prudentes et fatuae   V. Ciampi
L I-Vmc

203 1780   Coronatio Salomonis   A. Calegari
L I-Vcg *N* 'drama sacrum'

204 1782   Il ritorno di Tobia (C. Gozzi?)   B. Galuppi?
L I-Vcg; Rsc *N* I-Vcg has 'Incurabili' in ms; Rsc attrib. Galuppi in
catalogue

205 1784   Divinae hypostasis encomium   G. Cocchi
L I-Vcg *N* see no. 165

206 1785   Exitus Israel   M. Rauzzini
L I-Vcg

207 1785   Plagae Aegypti   M. Rauzzini
L I-Vcg

iii: Mendicanti (Ospedale dei Mendicanti)

208 1667   L'anima pentita   ?
L I-Mb; MOe *N* 'con cantata, prologo e intermedi per musica'

209 1682   Il fiore delle virtù christiane   ?
L I-Mb

210 1687   L'Erodiade ovvero La morte di   ?
                S Gio. Battista (G. B. Neri)
L I-BGc; Bca; Mb; Vcg; Nc; Vnm *N* singers' names in I-Vcg

211 1687   S. Giovanni decollato   ?
L I-BGc *N* perf. 29 Aug (PV)

212 1688   Tomaso Moro (G. B. Neri)   ?
L I-Vcg; Mb; RVI; Vnm *N* perf. Jan (PV)

213 1690   Davidis conversio   ?
L I-Vcg; Rsc *N* singers' names in I-Vcg

214 1691   Divinae gratiae triumphus intro-   ?
                ductio ad Salve regina
L I-Vcg

215 1693   Manassis captivitas   ?
L I-Vcg *N* ends 'sequitur psalmum Miserere'

216 1694   Patientia victrix sive Jobi patientia   ?
L I-Vcg; Rsc *N* ends with Miserere

217 1695   Squallidus florum luctus   ?
                (C. Joanellus)
L I-Vcg; La; Ma; Rsc; Vnm *N* ends with Miserere

No.	Date	Title (Librettist if known)	Composer
218	1703	Tomaso Moro (G. B. Neri)	N. Giovanardi
		N see no. 212; Girardi, p.171	
219	1706	Anima poenitens in psalmo	?
		Miserere	
	L I-Rsc		
220	1707	Christus bajulans crucem (B.	?
		Sandrinelli)	
	L I-Vcg; Rsc		
221	1710	Lazarus reviviscens	?
	L I-Vnm; Vcg; Rsc *N* singers' names in ms, I-Vnm		
222	1712	Humilitas exaltata	?
	L I-Vcg; Vmc *N* singers' names in ms, I-Vmc		
223	1713	Manhu tragedia sacra	?
	L I-Vcg *N* 'recitanda die dominica palmarum'		
224	1713	Supplices tragedia sacra	?
	L I-Vcg *N* perf. 22 July		
225	1717	Dei nati gloriae	?
	L I-Vcg; Vnm; Rsc *N* singers' names in ms, I-Rsc		
226	1717	Humilitas exaltata	?
	L I-Rsc; Vcg *N* see no. 222; singers' names in ms, I-Vcg		
227	1723	Tobias	?
	L I-Vcg		
228	1737	Sacra paraphrasis in psalmum	G. Saratelli
		Benedixisti	
	L I-Rsc		

(From here onwards, all librettos print singers' names.)

No.	Date	Title (Librettist if known)	Composer
229	1739	Magdalenae conversio (C. Gol-	G. Saratelli
		doni)	
	L I-Vcg; Rsc		
230	1740	Sancta Maria Magdalena	B. Galuppi
	L I-Vcg; Rsc *N* perf. 22 July		
231	1742	Prudens Abigail (Pasquali?)	B. Galuppi
	L I-Vcg; Vmc; Rsc *N* perf. 22 July		
232	1745	Isaac	B. Galuppi
	L I-Vcg; Rsc		
233	1746	Judith	B. Galuppi
	L I-Rsc		
234	1747-53?	Carmina praecinenda	?
	L I-Vcg *N* ends with Miserere; dated by singers		
235	1747	Jahel	B. Galuppi
	L I-Vcg; Vnm; Bu; PAc *S* Allgemeine Musikgesellschaft, Zurich		
236	1747	Rhythmi sacri	B. Galuppi
	L I-Rsc		
237	1748	Devoti affectus	B. Galuppi
	L I-Vmc; Vcg; Rsc; Bu		
238	1748	Devoti sacri	B. Galuppi
	L I-Bc; Rsc		
239	1748	Jahel	B. Galuppi
	L I-Rsc *N* see no. 235		

No.	Date	Title (Librettist if known)	Composer
240	1750	Aqua e rupe Horeb carmina praecinenda psalmo Miserere	B. Galuppi

L I-Vcg; Vmc; Rsc; Bu

| 241 | 1752 | Carmina praecinenda psalmo Miserere | ? |

L I-Vcg; Rsc *N* date in ms, I-Rsc

| 242 | 1752 | In festo S. Mariae Magdalenae | F. Bertoni |

L I-Rsc

| 243 | 1753 | Peregrinatio ad sanctum Domini | F. Bertoni |

L I-Vcg; Rsc *N* 'actio sacra'

| 244 | 1753 | Sacra modulamina | F. Bertoni |

L I-Vcg; Rsc *N* solo motets

| 245 | 1754 | In festo S. Mariae Magdalenae | F. Bertoni |

L I-Vcg; Nn *N* solo motets; pp. 13-16 'Co' stromenti, e con bassi'; pp. 22-4 'violini pizzicati'

| 246 | 1755 | Cum amore divino | F. Bertoni |

L I-Vmc

| 247 | 1755 | Modulamina sacra | F. Bertoni |

L I-Vcg

| 248 | 1756 | Modulamina sacra | F. Bertoni |

L I-Vcg; Rsc

| 249 | 1756 | De prodigo filio | F. Bertoni |

L I-Vcg; Rsc *S* I-Vnm

| 250 | 1757 | Modulamina sacra | F. Bertoni |

L I-Vcg; Rsc

| 251 | 1757 | Vaticinia prophetarum | F. Bertoni |

L I-Vcg; Rsc; US-Cn

| 252 | 1758 | Christus in sepulcro | F. Bertoni |

L I-Vcg; Rsc *N* ends with Miserere

| 253 | 1758 | Modulamina sacra | F. Bertoni |

L I-Vcg *N* solo motets

| 254 | 1759 | Longinus centurio | F. Bertoni |

L I-Vcg; Fm *N* ends with Miserere

| 255 | 1759 | Modulamina sacra | F. Bertoni |

L I-Vcg; Rsc *N* solo motets

| 256 | 1760 | Carmina sacra | F. Bertoni |

L I-Vcg; Rsc

| 257 | 1760 | Sermo discipulorum Christi in vespere diei parasceve sacra isagoge ad psalmum Miserere | F. Bertoni |

L I-Vcg; Rsc; Bc

| 258 | 1761 | Mater Jesu...sacra isagoge ad psalmum Miserere | F. Bertoni |

L I-Vcg; Rsc

| 259 | 1761 | Rythmi sacri | F. Bertoni |

L I-Vcg *N* solo motets

| 260 | 1762 | Maria Magdalenae apostola resurrectionis | F. Bertoni |

L I-Vcg; Rsc

| 261 | 1762 | Piae virgines choristae | F. Bertoni |

L I-Vcg; Vmc *N* minimal stage directions; ends with Miserere

No.	Date	Title (Librettist if known)	Composer

262 1763   Pium ascetarum colloquium   F. Bertoni
L I-Vcg; Vnm; Vc

263 1763   Rithmi sacri   F. Bertoni
L I-Vcg *N* solo motets

264 1764   Parasceve ad sepulturam   F. Bertoni
L I-Vnm; Vcg *N* minimal stage directions; ends with Miserere

265 1764   Sacer dialogus   F. Bertoni
L I-Vcg; Vnm *S* S-Skma

266 1765   Canenda musices carmina   ?
L I-Vcg (ms) *N* 'die solemnitatis Marie Magdalene vigesima secunda
mensis Julÿ'

267 1765   Secunda dies   F. Bertoni
L I-Vcg; Vnm *N* ends with Miserere

268 1766   Argumenta desumpta   F. Bertoni
L I-Vcg *N* solo motets

269 1766   Hortus in praedio   F. Bertoni
L I-Vcg; Vnm; Rsc *N* minimal stage directions?

270 1767   Hortus in praedio   F. Bertoni
L I-Vcg *N* same cast as no. 269

271 1767   Sacra carmina   F. Bertoni
L I-Vcg; Rsc *N* solo motets

272 1767   Tertia dies   F. Bertoni
L I-Vcg; Cini; Rsc *N* ends with Miserere

273 1768   Argumenta desumpta   F. Bertoni
L I-Vcg *N* solo motets

274 1768   Rex Assuerus   F. Bertoni
L I-Vcg; Cini; Vnm; Rsc; Bca; Bc *N* minimal stage directions?

275 1769   Divinae completae redemptionis F. Bertoni
L I-Vcg; Vnm; Rsc

276 1769   Modulamina sacra   F. Bertoni
L I-Vcg *N* solo motets

277 1769   Virtutum concordia   F. Bertoni
L I-Vcg

278 1770   Exitium primogenitorum Aegypti F. Bertoni
L I-Vcg *N* ends with Miserere

279 1770   Gloria et exaltatio fidei in   F. Bertoni
Abraham sacrificio
L I-Vcg; Vmc; Cini; Rsc

280 1771   Goliath   F. Bertoni
L I-Vcg; Vmc; Rsc *N* ends with Magnificat

281 1771   Jonathas   F. Bertoni
L I-Vcg; Cini; Rsc; PAc

282 1772   Profectio Moysis in Aegyptum   F. Bertoni
L I-Vcg; Rsc

283 1772   Salomon rex Israel   F. Bertoni
L I-Vcg; Rsc

284 1773   Susanna   F. Bertoni
L I-Vcg; Vmc; DK-Kk *N* Dk-Kk – text in Italian and Danish

285 1773   Tobias   F. Bertoni
L I-Vcg; Bc; Rsc; PAc

No.	Date	Title (Librettist if known)	Composer
286	1774?	Jephte sacrificium	G. Paisiello

L I-Vcg; Rsc *N* date in ms, I-Rsc

287	1774	Saul furens	F. Bertoni

L I-Vcg; Cini; Rsc

288	1775	David poenitens	F. Bertoni

L I-Vcg; Bc; Fm; Ma; Rsc; Cini *S* A-Wn; D-MÜs; F-Pc; I-Mc

289	1775	Interitus Absalon	F. Bertoni

L I-Vcg; Bc; Rsc

290	1776	Joas rex Juda	F. Bertoni

L I-Vcg; Cini; Fm; Pu; PAc; Rsc *S* D-Dlb

291	1777	Abigail	F. Bertoni

L I-Vcg; Vmc; Rsc

292	1777	Canticorum sponsa	F. Bertoni

L I-Vcg; Vmc

293	1778	Nabal	F. Bertoni

L I-Vcg *N* re-working of no. 291

294	1779	Athaliae mors	F. Bertoni

L I-Vcg; Rsc; Ma

295	1779	Poenitentia David	F. Bertoni

L I-Vcg *N* similar to no. 288

296	1779	Sacer dialogus	?

L I-Vmc *N* dialogue between Achinoam and Jonathas followed by Salve regina

297	1779	Victoria militum David	F. Bertoni

L I-Vcg

298	1780	Bethulia liberata	F. Alessandri

L I-Vcg *S* I-Pca

299	1780	De morte Sisarae	G. Avanzini

L I-Vcg

300	1780	Tres pueri Hebrei	F. Bianchi

S I-Vsm

301	1781	Samson	F. Piticchio

L I-Vcg; Vmc

302	1781	Balthassar	F. Bertoni

L I-Vcg; Vmc *S* I-Mc *N* score in I-Mc as revived 1784 as Abraham e Balthasar. This and the following oratorios of 1781 were advertised in the 'Avviso'. See chapter 4, n. 7

303	1781	Bethulia liberata	F. Alessandri

N see no. 298

304	1781	Canticorum sponsa	F. Bertoni
305	1781	Mors Athaliae	F. Bertoni

N see no. 294

306	1781	De morte Sisarae	G. Avanzini

N see no. 299

307	1781	Poenitentia David	F. Bertoni

N see no. 295

308	1781	Sacer dialogus: Jonathas	F. Bertoni
309	1782	Bethulia liberata	F. Alessandri

L I-Vcg *N* see no. 298

310	1782	De filio prodigo	P. Anfossi

L I-Vcg *S* I-Gi(l)

No.	Date	Title (Librettist if known)	Composer
311	1782	Sedecias	P. Anfossi
	L I-Vcg; Vmc *S* I-Bc; Mc; Rco		
312	1782	Somnium pharaonis	A. Pio
	L I-Vcg		
313	1783	Abraham sacrificium	F. Bianchi
	L I-Vcg; Vmc *S* I-Vsm		
314	1783	De filio prodigo	P. Anfossi
	L I-Vcg; Vmc *N* see no. 310; slightly different libretto		
315	1783	Triumphus David de Goliat gigante	G. Mauroceno
	L I-Vcg; Vmc *N* 4 singers, but three sing 2 characters each		
316	1783	Sedecias	P. Anfossi
	L I-Vcg		
317	1784	Balthassar	F. Bertoni
	L I-Vcg *N* see no. 302		
318	1784	Canticorum sponsa	F. Bertoni
	L I-Vcg; Vmc *N* see no. 292		
319	1784	Salome mater Machabea	L. Baini
	L I-Vcg; Vmc; Cini; Rsc		
320	1784	Sedecias	P. Anfossi
	L I-Vcg; Vmc *N* see no. 311; but cast much smaller		
321	1785	Agar fugiens	F. Bianchi
	L I-Vcg; Vmc *S* D-SWl; F-Pc; I-Mc		
322	1785	Jephte Galaadites	G. Valentini
	L I-Vcg; Vmc; Cini; Rsc		
323	1785	Sisara	F. Bertoni
	N NG		
324	1786	Absalonis rebellio	G. Avanzini
	L I-Vcg; Vmc; Rsc		
325	1786	Jephte Galaadites	G. Valentini
	L I-Pu *N* see no. 322		
326	1787	Canticorum sponsa	F. Bertoni
	N Zorzi 36		
327	1787	Ninive conversa	P. Anfossi
	L I-Vcg; Rsc *S* GB-Lbm (Part I); I-Mc		
328	1786	Moyses de Horeb revertens	G. Valentini
	L I-Vmc; Rsc		
329	1787?	Nuptiae Rachelis	A. Brunetti
	L I-Vcg		
330	1787	Susanna	G. Gazzaniga
	L I-Vcg; Fm; Pu; PAc; Cini		
331	1788	Humanae fragilitatis	G. Gazzaniga
	L I-Vcg; Pu		
332	1788	Sedecias	P. Anfossi
	L I-Pu *S* I-Bc; Mc; Rco *N* 4 singers, each taking 2 parts; see no. 316		
333	1788	Susanna	G. Gazzaniga
	L I-Vcg; Rsc *N* see no. 330		
334	1789	Abigail	A. Favi
	L I-Vcg; Pu		
335	1789?	Solemne Saulis	G. Valentini
	L I-Vcg; Pu; Rsc		

No.	Date	Title (Librettist if known)	Composer
336	1789	Joseph a fratribus agnitus	G. Sarti
		L I-Vcg; PAc; Rsc; Pu; Cini	
337	1789	Ninive conversa	P. Anfossi
		L I-Vcg; Rsc; Pu N see no. 327	
338	1790	Abimelech	F. A. de Blasis
		L I-Vmc; Cini; Rsc	
339	1790	Joas rex Juda	F. Bianchi
		L I-Vcg; Pu; Rsc S F-Pc; I-Mc	
340	1790	Ninive conversa	P. Anfossi
		L I-Vcg; Rsc; Fm; Fn N see no. 327	
341	1791	Jacob a Labano fugiens	S. Mayr
		L I-Rsc	
342	1791	Jerico diruta	P. Anfossi
		L I-Pu S I-Mc N score in I-Mc as Jerico distrutta	
343	1792	Esther	V. Manfredini
		L I-Vcg; Rsc; Fm	
344	1792	Maria quaerit	J. Haydn
		L I-Vcg; Vmc N for Bianca Sacchetti for Mendicanti?	
345	1792	Susanna	G. Gazzaniga
		L I-Fm; Mb; Vmc N see no. 333	
346	1793	Machabeorum mater	D. Fischietti
		L I-Vcg	
347a	1793	Le nozze di Ruth	I. Girace
		L I-Vcg N ms libretto	
347b	1793	Nuptiae Ruth	I. Girace
		L I-Rsc; Cini	
348	1793	Sisara	S. Mayr
		L I-Vcg; Vmc; Pu; Rsc; Cini	
349	1794	Jacob a Labano fugiens	S. Mayr
		L I-Vcg N see no. 341	
350	1794	Sisara	S. Mayr
		L I-Fm N see no. 348	
351	1794	Tobiae matrimonium	S. Mayr
		L I-Rsc; Pu; Cini	
352	1795	David in spelunca Engaddi	S. Mayr
		L I-Vcg; Rsc; PAc	
353	1796	Abraham sacrificium	F. Gardi
		L I-Vcg; Vnm; Rsc	
354	1796	Jephte	F. Antonolini
		L I-Vmc; Cini; Rsc	
355	1797	Ninive conversa	P. Anfossi?
		L I-Vmc; Vc; Rsc N repeat of no. 327?	

iv: Ospedaletto (Ospedale dei Poveri Derelitti)

No.	Date	Title (Librettist if known)	Composer
356	1716	Sacrum amoris novendiale (G. Cassetti)	A. Pollarolo
		L I-Vcg; Vnm; Rsc	
357	1717	Rosa inter spinas (G. Cassetti)	A. Pollarolo
		L I-Rsc	

No.	Date	Title (Librettist if known)	Composer
358	1717	Sterilis faecunda (G. Cassetti)	A. Pollarolo
	L I-Vcg		

(From here onwards, all librettos print singers' names.)

359	1747	Modulamina sacra	A. G. Pampani

L I-Rsc; Bc *N* solo motets for Mass and Vespers with concertos for violin and cello

360	1748	Modulamina sacra	A. G. Pampani

L I-Vcg *N* as for no. 359

361	1749	Rhythmi sacri	A. G. Pampani

L I-Vcg; Rsc *N* as for no. 359

362	1750	Rhythmi sacri	A. G. Pampani

L I-Vcg *N* solo motets

363	1751	Musicales rhythmi	A. G. Pampani

L I-Vcg; Rsc *N* solo motets

364	1752	Recurrente festo deiparae in coelum	A. G. Pampani

L I-Rsc *N* solo motets

365	1753	Carmina sacra	A. G. Pampani

L I-Vcg *N* solo motets with concertos for violin and cello, names written as well as printed

366	1754	Carmina sacra	A. G. Pampani

L I-Vcg *N* solo motets with concerto for cello

367	1754	Messiae praeconium carmine complexum	A. G. Pampani

L I-Vcg; Rsc *N* libretto incl. advertisement by printer A. Groppo

368	1755	Carmina sacra	A. G. Pampani

L I-Vcg *N* solo motets, concertos for violin, cello, viola d'amore; Groppo advertisement as for no. 367

369	1755	Sofonea idest Joseph pro rex Aegypti	A. G. Pampani

L I-Vcg *N* 'drama sacrum'

370	1756	Carmina sacra	A. G. Pampani

L I-Rsc

371	1757	Triumphus Judith	A. G. Pampani

L I-Rsc; Vcg *N* ends with carmina sacra incl. a cello concerto

372	1758	Carmen sacrum	A. G. Pampani

L I-Vcg

373	1758	Sacrorum carminum contexta corolla	A. G. Pampani

L I-Rsc *N* solo motets

374	1760	Prophetiae evangelicae ac mors Isaiae	A. G. Pampani

L I-Rsc; Vcg

375	1761	Concentus armonici	A. G. Pampani

L I-Rsc *N* 'dialogue' leading to solo motets

376	1761	Gesù presentato al tempio	A. Sacchini

S A-Wn *N* perf. Venice?

377	1764	Pro solemni die B.V.M.	A. G. Pampani

L I-Vcg *N* solo motets

No.	Date	Title (Librettist if known)	Composer
378	1764	Rex Salomon (D. Benedetti)	T. Traetta
	L I-Vcg; IRE; Vc; Nc; Ma S *B-Br		
379	1766	Rex Salomon (D. Benedetti)	T. Traetta
	L I-Vcg N see no. 378		
380	1767?	Carmina sacra	A. Sacchini
	L I-Vcg N dated from when singers employed		
381	1767-74?	Carmina sacra	A. Sacchini
	L I-Vcg N dated from when singers employed		
382	1767	Carmen sacrum	T. Traetta
	L I-Vcg N solo motets		
383	1767	Pulchra ut luna (P. Chiari)	T. Traetta
	L I-Vmc; Cini; Rsc		
384	1769	Rex Salomon	T. Traetta
	L I-Vcg N see no. 378		
385	1769	In solemni triduo in honorem Divi Hieronymi Aemiliani	A. Sacchini
	L I-Vcg N 'celebrando diebus 16.17.18 Aprilis' *followed by*		
386		Charitas omnia vincit	A. Sacchini
	L I-Vcg; Vnm; Cini; Rsc		
387	1770	Machabeorum mater (P. Chiari)	A. Sacchini
	L I-Vcg; Vc; IRE; Cini; Rsc		
388	1771	Carmina sacra	A. Sacchini
	L I-Vcg N solo motets		
389	1771	Jephtes sacrificium (P. Chiari)	A. Sacchini
	L I-Vcg; Vc; IRE; Cini		
390	1772	Nuptiae Ruth (P. Chiari)	A. Sacchini
	L I-Vcg; Vc; Cini; IRE; Rsc; Pu N ends 'in Missa solemni'		
391.	1773	Carmina sacra	P. Anfossi
	L I-Vcg; Vc; IRE N solo motets		
392	1773	Noe sacrificium (P. Chiari)	P. Anfossi
	L I-Vmc; Vcg; Fm; Cini S I-Vc; Pca		
393	1774	Jerusalem eversa (P. Chiari)	P. Anfossi
	L I-Vcg; Vmc; Fn		
394	1775	Carmina sacra	P. Anfossi
	L I-Vcg N solo motets 'die 9 Julii'		
395	1775	David contra Philistaeos (P. Chiari)	P. Anfossi
	L I-Vcg; Vmc; Bc; Pu; Rsc; Cini; Fm; Fn		
396	1776	Carmina sacra	P. Anfossi
	L I-Vcg; Rsc		
397	1776	Rex Salomon	T. Traetta
	L I-Vcg N see no. 378		
398	1777	Samuelis umbra (P. Chiari)	P. Anfossi
	L I-Vcg; Cini: Rsc; Fn		
399	1778	Carmina sacra	P. Anfossi
	L I-Vcg N 'Erit iterum 8 Septembris'		
400	1780	Tobiae reditus ad patrem	P. Anfossi
	L I-Vcg N 'actio sacra'		
401	1780	Virginis assumptae triumphus	P. Anfossi
	L I-Vcg; Vmc; Rsc N 'actio sacra'		

No.	Date	Title (Librettist if known)	Composer
402	1781	Esther	P. Anfossi
		L I-Vcg S I-Bc N 'actio sacra'	
403	1781	Esther	J. Schuster
		L I-Vcg; Vmc; Fm; PAc; Rsc; Vnm	
404	1782	Absalom	D. Cimarosa
		L I-Vcg; Rsc; Rn; Fm S D-Dlb; MÜs; F-Pn; GB-Lbm; *I-Nc	
405	1782?	Giuditta (P. Bagnoli)	D. Cimarosa
		S A-Wgm (as Judith); I-Nc; I-Fc and F-Pn (as Betulia)	
406	1782	Pharisaei conversio	F. Piticchio
		L I-Vcg S D-Dlb	
407	1783	Holophernes	O. C. Kospoth
		L I-Vcg; Vmc; Cini; PAc N 'actio sacra'	
408	1783	Primum fatale homicidium	G. Avanzini
		L I-Vcg; Vmc; Mb; Rsc	
409	1784	Philistaei a Jonatha dispersit	V. Martín y Soler
		L I-Vcg; Rsc N composer named as Vincentio Martini	
410	1785	Judith	G. Nicolini
		L I-Vmc; Rsc N 'actio sacra'	
411	1785	Grande Balthassar	G. Valentini
		L I-Vcg; Cini; Rsc	
412	1786	Nuptiae Jacobis	L. Baini
		L I-Vcg; Vnm N 'actio sacra'	
413	1787	Rebecca	F. Gardi
		L I-Vcg; Vmc N 'actio sacra'	
414	1787	Seba	F. Gardi
		L I-Vcg; Vmc N 'actio sacra'	
415	1788	Jerusalem eversa	P. Anfossi
		L I-Vmc N see no. 393	
416	1788	Salomon	F. Gardi
		L I-Vcg; Cini; Fm N 'actio sacra'	
417	1789	Abraham sacrificium	F. Gardi
		L I-Vcg; Vnm; Cini N 'actio sacra'	
418	1790	Amnom ab Absolone proditus	F. A. de Blasis
		followed by Mulier Thecutis	
		L I-Vcg; Vmc	
419	1791	Moyses ab aqua extractus	F. Gardi
		L I-Vcg N 'actio sacra'	

v: Pietà (Ospedale della Pietà)
(only singers' Christian names ever given)

No.	Date	Title (Librettist if known)	Composer
420	1683	La Maddalena che va all'Eremo	?
		L I-Rsc	
421	1684	Il giuditio universale (B. Sandrinelli)	?
		L I-Vnm	
422	1685	La Maddalena che va all'Eremo	?
		L I-Vcg N see no. 420	

No.	Date	Title (Librettist if known)	Composer
423	1687	Santa Maria egittiaca penitente (B. Sandrinelli)	G. Spada
	L I-Vcg *N* composer from PV		
424	1694	Altissimum verbi	?
	L I-Vcg		
425	1700	Humana natura reparata (B. Sandrinelli)	?
	L I-Vcg; Rsc		
426	1701	Triumphas misericordiae (B. Sandrinelli)	F. Gasparini
	L I-Vmc; Rsc		
427	1702	Prima culpa per redemptionem deleta (B. Sandrinelli)	F. Gasparini
	L I-Rsc		
428	1703	Jubilum prophetarum (B. Sandrinelli)	F. Gasparini
	L I-Rsc; Vcg; Vnm		
429	1704	Aeterna sapientia incarnata (B. Sandrinelli)	F. Gasparini
	L I-Rsc; Vcg		
430	1705	Pudor virginis vindicatus	F. Gasparini
	L I-Rsc		
431	1706	Genus humanum	F. Gasparini
	L I-Vcg *N* singers' names in ms		
432	1706?	Sol in tenebris	F. Gasparini
	L I-Vnm		
433	1708	Dominicae nativitatis praeludium	F. Gasparini
	L I-Vmc		
434	1711	Glorioso redentore	F. Gasparini?
	N PV		
435	1711	Maria Magdalene videns Christum	F. Gasparini
	L I-Rsc; Vc; Vnm		
436	1712	Moisè liberato dal Nilo	F. Gasparini
	L I-Vcg		
437	1714	Maria Magdalene	F. Gasparini
	L I-Vnm *N* singers' names in ms; different libretto from no. 435		
438	1714	Moyses Deus pharaonis	A. Vivaldi
	L I-Rsc; Vcg; Pu *N* singers' names in ms, I-Vcg		
439	1714	Tobias redux	?
	L I-Rsc; Vcg		
440	1716	Juditha triumphans (G. Cassetti)	A. Vivaldi
	L I-Rsc; Vcg *S* I-Tn		
441	1717	Anima rediviva	F. Gasparini
	N PV		
442	1717	Maria Magdalena	F. Gasparini
	N PV		
443	1736	Innocentiae triumphus	G. Porta
	L I-Vcg; Rsc		
444	1744	Davidis lapsus	A. Bernasconi
	L I-Vcg; Rsc		

No.	Date	Title (Librettist if known)	Composer

(From here onwards, most librettos print singers' names.)

| 445 | 1746 | Adonais | A. Bernasconi |

L I-Vcg; Rsc; Bca *N* 'drama sacrum'

| 446 | 1746 | Pastorum dialogus in Domini nativitate | A. Bernasconi |

L I-Vcg; Rsc

| 447 | 1747 | Jonathas | A. Bernasconi |

L I-Vcg; Cini; Rsc *N* 'drama sacrum'

| 448 | 1751 | David | A. Bernasconi |

L I-Vcg; Rsc *N* 'drama sacrum'

| 449 | 1752 | Carmina canenda | A. Bernasconi |

L I-Rsc *N* solo motets

| 450 | 1755 | Sanctorum patrum in Abrahae | C. Latilla |

L I-Vcg

| 451 | 1756 | Carmina sacra | C. Latilla |

L I-Rsc *N* solo motets

| 452 | 1757 | Judith triumphans | C. Latilla |

L I-Rsc

| 453 | 1760 | Modulamina sacra | C. Latilla |

L I-Vcg *N* 'dialogum sacrum'

| 454 | 1761 | Sacra Esther historia | C. Latilla |

L I-Vcg

| 455 | 1766 | Sacer dialogus David inter et Salomonem | G. Sarti |

L I-Vcg

| 456 | 1768 | Joseph pro-rex Aegypti | B. Furlanetto |

L I-Vcg *S* I-Vc (1811) *N* minimal stage directions

| 457 | 1768 | Primum fatale homicidium | G. Sciroli |

N Zorzi 200a

| 458 | 1768 | Vexillum redemptionis exaltatum | S. Perillo |

L I-Vcg *N* ends with Magnificat

| 459 | 1770 | De nativitate virginis | B. Furlanetto |

L I-Vcg; Rsc *S* I-Vc *N* I-Vc score 'Oratorio secondo'

| 460 | 1771 | Moyses in Nilo | B. Furlanetto |

L I-Vmc; Rsc *S* I-Vc (1797)

| 461 | 1773 | Athalia | B. Furlanetto |

L I-Vcg *S* I-Vc

| 462 | 1773 | Felix Victoria | B. Furlanetto |

N NG

| 463 | 1773 | Jaelis victoria | B. Furlanetto |

L I-Vcg; Vnm *S* I-Vc *N* singers' names in ms, I-Vc

| 464 | 1773 | Modi sacri | B. Furlanetto |

L I-Vcg *N* ends with 'Alma redemptoris'

| 465 | 1773-4? | Vitae calamitates | B. Furlanetto |

N Zorzi 304

| 466 | 1774 | Templi reparatio | B. Furlanetto |

L I-Vcg; Vmc *S* I-Vc (1813)

| 467 | 1775 | Carmina sacra | B. Furlanetto |

L I-Vcg *N* ends with 'Alma redemptoris'

No.	Date	Title (Librettist if known)	Composer
468	1775	Jerico	B. Furlanetto
	L I-Vcg *S* I-Vc (1795)		
469	1776	David in Siceleg	B. Furlanetto
	L I-Vcg *S* I-Vc (parts)		
470	1777	Carmen sacer	B. Furlanetto
	L I-Vcg (ms) *N* ends with 'Salve regina'		
471	1777	Israelis liberatio	B. Furlanetto
	L I-Vcg		
472	1777	Mors Adam	B. Furlanetto
	L I-Vmc *S* I-Vc (1809)		
473	1777	Reditus exercitus Israelitici	B. Furlanetto
	L I-Vcg; Vmc; Ma *S* I-Vc (Part I only) *N* 2 versions of libretto		
474	1778	Naboth	B. Furlanetto
	L I-Vcg *S* I-Vc; Pca		
475	1779	De filio prodigo	B. Furlanetto
	L I-Vcg; Vmc *S* I-Vc (1800)		
476	1779	Somnium pharaonis	B. Furlanetto
	L I-Vcg; Vmc		
477	1780	David Goliath triumphator	B. Furlanetto
	L I-Vcg *S* I-Vc (1802)		
478	1780	Dies extrema mundi	B. Furlanetto
	L I-Vcg		
479	1780	Sacer dialogus	B. Furlanetto
	N between 'Anima sancta' and 'Anima rea'; Zorzi 219		
480	1781	Jonathas	B. Furlanetto
	L I-Vcg; Vmc; Cini *S* I-Vc (1798)		
481	1782	Salomon rex Israel	B. Furlanetto
	L I-Vcg; Vnm *S* I-Vc (1806)		
482	1783	Aurea statua a rege Nabuco-donosor	B. Furlanetto
	S I-Vc (1803) *N* NG		
483	1783	Reditus exercitus Israelitici	B. Furlanetto
	L I-Vcg *N* see no. 473		
484	1784	Prudens Abigail	B. Furlanetto
	L I-Vcg *S* I-Vc		
485	1785	Absalonis rebellio	B. Furlanetto
	L I-Vcg *S* I-Vc		
486	1785	In coelo resplendet	B. Furlanetto
	S I-Vc		
487	1785	Jerico	B. Furlanetto
	L I-Vmc; Rsc *S* I-Vc (1795) *N* see no. 468		
488	1785	Moyses ad Rubum	B. Furlanetto
	L I-Vcg		
489	1786	Abraham et Isach	B. Furlanetto
	L I-Vcg; Pci *S* I-Vc		
490	1786	Sisara	B. Furlanetto
	L I-Vmc *S* I-Vc		
491	1787	Judith triumphans	B. Furlanetto
	L I-Vnm *S* I-Vc		
492	1787	De solemni Balthassar	B. Furlanetto
	L I-Vmc *S* I-Vc		

No.	Date	Title (Librettist if known)	Composer
493	1788	De solemni nuptiae in domum Labani	B. Furlanetto
	L I-Vcg *S* I-Vc (1797)		
494	1789	De solemni Balthassar	B. Furlanetto
	L I-Vcg		
495	1789	Triumphus Jephte	B. Furlanetto
	L I-Vcg *S* I-Vc *N* minimal stage directions?		
496	1790	Bethulia liberata	B. Furlanetto
	L I-Vmc; Rsc *S* I-Vc (1804)		
497	1792	Gedeon	B. Furlanetto
	L I-Vcg; Vmc *S* I-Vc (1793)		
498	1795	Jerico	B. Furlanetto
	S I-Vc *N* see no. 468		
499	1795	Nuptiae Rachelis	B. Furlanetto
	S I-Vc		
500	1797	Moyses in Nilo	B. Furlanetto
	L I-Pci *S* I-Vc *N* see no. 460		
501	1797	De solemni nuptiae in domo Labani	B. Furlanetto
	S I-Vc		
502	1798	Jonathas	B. Furlanetto
	L I-Vcg; Mb; PESo *S* I-Vc *N* see no. 480		
503	1800	De filio prodigo	B. Furlanetto
	S I-Vc *N* see no. 475		
504	1800	Primum fatale homicidium	B. Furlanetto
	L I-Rsc		
505	1801	Triumphus Jephte	B. Furlanetto
	L I-Vcg *S* I-Vc *N* see no. 495		
506	1802	David Goliath triumphator	B. Furlanetto
	S I-Vc *N* see no. 477		
507	1803	Aurea statua	B. Furlanetto
	S I-Vc *N* see no. 482		
508	1803	David Goliath triumphator	B. Furlanetto
	S I-Vc (1802) *N* see no. 477		
509	1804	Bethulia liberata	B. Furlanetto
	S I-Vc *N* see no. 496		
510	1804	Salomon	B. Furlanetto
	L I-Vnm *S* I-Vc (1806) *N* see no. 481		
511	1805	Felix victoria	B. Furlanetto
	S I-Vc		
512	1805	Jaelis victoria	B. Furlanetto
	S I-Vc *N* see no. 463		
513	1806	David Goliath	B. Furlanetto
	S I-Vc *N* see no. 477		
514	1806	Salomon	B. Furlanetto
	S I-Vc *N* see no. 481		
515	1807	Prudens Abigail	B. Furlanetto
	L I-Vcg *S* I-Vc *N* see no. 484		
516	1808	Jephte	B. Furlanetto
	N Caffi; see no. 495		

No.	Date	Title (Librettist if known)	Composer
517	1809	Joseph pro-rex Aegypti	B. Furlanetto
	L I-Vmc		

vi: Miscellaneous

518	1662	La vergine in Egitto (B. Sandrinelli)	?

N Allacci

519	1675	S. Catterina d'Alessandria	?

L I-Vnm; Mb; Rsc; RVI; US-LAu   *N* Act I 'Massentio sopra carro tirato da Christiani incatenati, che passa sopra i cadaveri'

520	1681	La sommersione di Faraone	?

L I-Vcg   *N* perf. at S. Giorgio Maggiore

521	1683	Abramo vincitore	G. A. Perti

S I-MOe   *N* NG

522	1685	Il cuore umano al'incanto (Mons. Petrucci)	G. A. Manara

L I-Mb

523	1694	Le finezze d'amore (G. Zuanelli)	?

L I-Vcm   *N* perf. at 'Chiesa della Santissima Ascensione'

524	1696	L'Abigaille	?

L Los Angeles, public library   *N* 'a cinque con istromenti del Sig. Bernardo Caffi'

525	1696	Atalia	?

L I-Vnm   *N* for 'Principe Altieri'

526	1697	I quindici misteri del santissimo rosario	?

L I-Mb   *N* perf. 'nell' Ascensione'

527	1698	Il finto Esau	?

L Cini   *N* for perf. during Carnival by the pupils of G. Fianello

528	1699	Il martirio di S. Adriano	F. A. Pistocchi

L I-Mb; BGc   *S* I-MOe   *N* perf. at SS Giovanni e Paolo

529	1700	Conversione di Cassano re d'Armenia (L. Alberici d'Orvieto)	?

N Allacci

530	1700	Ghirlanda di divozione... di quindici mistiche rose	?

N perf. at 'Chiesa dell'Ascensione'; Allacci

531	1700	Il martirio de' Santi Didimo e Teodora (L. Alberici d'Orvieto)	?

N Allacci

532	1701	Giuditta guerriera (F. Tomassini)	?

L I-Vnm   *N* stage directions

533	1702	Clemenza di Salamone (G. F. Roberti)	C. F. Pollarolo

N Allacci; NG

534	1702	Jefte	C. F. Pollarolo

L B-Bc; I-Rsc   *S* A-Wn

535	1702	I pensieri divoti (G. F. Roberti)	C. A. Badia

N 'cantati nel Palazzo Apostolico'

No.	Date	Title (Librettist if known)	Composer
536	1709	Adorationis tributa nascenti Domino	?
		L I-Rsc	
537	1709	Oratorio...da cantarsi nella ven. compagnia della purificazione di Maria Vergine	F. Gasparini
		N Allacci	
538	1710	Agonia del glorioso S. Giuseppe (L. Alberici d'Orvieto)	?
		N Allacci	
539	1710	La Giuditta (B. Marcello)	B. Marcello
		L I-Vcg	
540	1727	S. Romualdo (R. Merighi)	?
		L I-Mb; Pu; Rsc; Vnm; D-Mbs *N* for 7th centenary of saint's death	
541	1727	Joaz (A. Zeno)	B. Marcello?
		L I-Vnm *N* I-Vnm in ms: 'posta in musica dal Sig. Benedetto Marcello'	
542	1729	La fuga dal secolo di S. Romoaldo	?
		L I-Mb; Cini; D-Mth *N* libretto in Cini: perf. at Murano	
543	1731	Giaele (D. Giupponi)	D. Bigaglia
		N perf. at S. Giorgio Maggiore; Allacci	
544	1731	Il pianto e il riso delle quattro stagioni (G. Viteschelli?)	B. Marcello
		S *GB-Lbm *N* NG Venice?	
545	1732	La passione di Gesù Cristo (P. Metastasio)	?
		L I-Mb; Ma	
546	1733	Abramo (D. Lalli)	?
		L I-Mb; Rsc	
547	1733	Leudaclo e Tosi	N. Porpora
		N Allacci	
548	1733?	Il trionfo della poesia e della musica (G. Viteschelli?)	B. Marcello
		S B-Bc	
549	1736	Il peccato originale (D. Lalli)	?
		N Allacci	
550	1737	Li dolori della SS. Vergine (D. Lalli)	?
		L I-Vnm	
551	1738	L'Abel (D. Lalli)	?
		L I-Vnm	
552	1746	Il peccato originale (D. Lalli)	?
		L I-Vnm	
553	1749	La passione di Gesù Cristo	Z. Cornaro
		L I-Rsc; Vcg	
554	1750	Oratorio a due voci nel celebrarsi le glorie del B. Giuseppe Calasanzio (G. Barsotti)	D. Gallo
		L I-Vmc *N* for 'un'Accademia di Lettere' at S. Lorenzo, Murano	
555	1752	Cantata per l'assunzione	?
		L Lucca, Biblioteca governativa *N* for S. Lorenzo, Murano	

No.	Date	Title (Librettist if known)	Composer
556	1754	Cantata...per la felice esaltazione ...di Torcello di Mons. N. A. Giustiniani	A. Bergamo
		L I-Mb; Rn	
557	1755	Il transito del giusto (A. Bianchi)	?
		L I-Mb	
558	1756	Sant'Elena al Calvario (P. Metastasio)	L. Leo
		L I-Mb; Vcg	
559	1758	La morte di Abele (P. Metastasio)	A. Pampani
		L I-Vcg; Mb	
560	1759?	L'unzione di Davidde (C. Goldoni)	?
		L Cini N 'Nuova Chiesa della Dottrina Christiana'	
561	1760	Il vitello d'oro (A. Bianchi)	?
		L I-Vcg N stage directions	
562	1765	Giubilo celeste (M. Fiecco)	B. Furlanetto
		L I-Vcg; Vnm N for parish church of S. Polo	
563	1766	Giubilo celeste (M. Fiecco)	B. Furlanetto
		L I-Mb N same libretto as no. 562	
564	1767	Componimento sacro per musica del Signore N.N.	S. Perillo
		L I-Vcg	
565	1767	Il trionfo del invitissimo proto-martire Giovanni Nepomuceno (M. Fiecco)	B. Furlanetto
		L I-Vnm	
566	1778	La passione di Gesù Cristo	G. Morosini
		L I-TSmt	
567	1781	La Betulia liberata (P. Metastasio)	G. Morosini
		L I-Vcg	
568	1782	Giuseppe riconosciuto (P. Metastasio)	G. Morosini
		L I-Mb; Rsc	
569	1789	Sedecia	?
		L I-Vcg N stage directions, chorus important, for the Accademia de' Rinnovati	
570	n. d.	Adorazione de' Magi (A. Abati)	?
		N Allacci	
571	n. d.	Santa Margherita	?
		N Allacci	
572	n. d.	Oratorio dedicato all'illustrissima et eccellentissima Signora Foscarini Nani	?
		L I-Vcg; Mb	
573	n. d.	Sant'Elena al Calvario (P. Metastasio)	G. Morosini
		L I-Vcg	

Index of Singers

This index records all the solo singers named in librettos or scores of oratorios performed at the Ospedali. References are to the serial numbers in the preceding list.

Mendicanti

Ospedaletto

Pietà

Index of Oratorios

All numbers in this index refer to entries in the Appendix.

General Index

The numbers in italics refer to the Appendix.
* indicates that there are one or more musical examples on the
page.